THE DARK SIDE OF INJURY:

NAVIGATING WORKER'S COMPENSATION, HEALTH INSURANCE, AND THE MEDICAL-PHARMACEUTICAL INDUSTRY

TOOLS FOR PROTECTING YOURSELF AND YOUR FAMILY

THE DARK SIDE OF INJURY:

NAVIGATING WORKER'S COMPENSATION, HEALTH INSURANCE, AND THE MEDICAL-PHARMACEUTICAL INDUSTRY

TOOLS FOR PROTECTING YOURSELF AND YOUR FAMILY

DEBRA MUTH
WHNP, ND, BSN, MSNH, BAAHP

MavenMark Books
Milwaukee, Wisconsin

Published by
MavenMark Books
An imprint of HenschelHAUS Publishing, Inc.
2625 S. Greeley St. Suite 201
Milwaukee, Wisconsin 53207
www.henschelHAUSbooks.com

ISBN: 978159598-315-2
E-ISBN: 978159598-316-9
Library of Congress Control Number: 2014938951

Publisher's Cataloging-In-Publication Data
(Prepared by The Donohue Group, Inc.)

Muth, Debra.
The dark side of injury : navigating worker's compensation, health insurance, and the medical-pharmaceutical industry : tools for protecting yourself and your family / Debra Muth, WHNP, ND, BSN, MSNH, BAAHP.

pages : illustrations ; cm

Issued also as an ebook.
Includes bibliographical references.
ISBN: 978-1-59598-315-2

1. Patient advocacy--United States. 2. Medical care--United States. 3. Workers' compensation--United States. 4. Health insurance--United States. 5. Physicians--Malpractice--United States. 6. Finance, Personal. I. Title.

R727.45 .M88 2014
362.10973   2014938951

Cover design by Express Creative.

Images used with permission from ScienceSource.

DEDICATION AND ACKNOWLEDGMENTS

I would like to thank my husband, Dennis. Without him, I would not have had the strength to write this book.

To my mom, who has always been there always believed in me, and has provided support to Dennis and me in more ways than I can list.

To our children, who have been patient and understanding with the life changes we have endured and never treated their father differently; they have accepted and loved him unconditionally.

To my friend, Sue Ogrezovich. Without her strength, support, and kindness, I would never have made it through the crazy roller-coaster ride we took. I have never thanked her enough for being there for me.

To my friend, Debbie Ellinger, who drove Dennis to his first medical appointment, encouraged me to tell my story, and has always believed in me.

To my friend, Sherrie Palm, who spent countless hours editing this book for me, and let me bend her ear whenever I needed to.

Thank you to all the people in my life who have made this book possible and helped me create a better life, and the many friends who have supported me, listened to me cry, and picked me up when I was down. Without their support, I would never have made it through these past few years.

All my love,
Debra

TABLE OF CONTENTS

TOOLS FOR PROTECTING YOURSELF AND YOUR FAMILY

Appendix:

PREFACE

On September 11, 2006, my husband Dennis injured his back at work, lifting a 200-pound turret, something he did every day. Dennis had never had a back injury or even a backache. That single movement changed our lives forever.

I am a nurse practitioner with an independent practice caring for patients with chronic illness using an integrative approach to healing. My education includes a Bachelor's degree in nursing, along with two years of training in the field of women's health to become a certified nurse practitioner. I completed my Master's degree in Natural Health and earned a Ph.D. in Naturopathic Medicine. This training has allowed me to look at patient's health using an integrative approach to medicine. I look for the cause of the problem instead of treating the symptoms.

My husband's boss thought he would improve his position in the company by saving the owners money—not such a bad idea, right? The problem occurred when he saved money by illegally avoiding filing worker's compensation claims. Many times, this is the first reason employers do not file a worker's compensation claim. Money is truly the root of all evil (or perhaps, it's greed?)

After my husband's injury, we received a quick lesson in the Unites States' Worker's Compensation program. It did not take long for us to also learn how the American legal system works when one files for medical malpractice.

Dennis and I used to believe in our worker's compensation system, the insurance industry, the legal system, and my own healthcare profession. My husband and I are honest people who followed the rules and thought his employer and employer's insurance would be held accountable. Nothing could have been farther from the truth!

We thought we could trust our doctor to do the right thing for us, not the right thing for his pocketbook and his own career at my husband's expense. We also discovered that the donation of a loved one's tissues and cells for transplant was nothing more than big business as well.

My hope is that this book provides you with information, words of advice, and new hope for you or a loved one during a difficult situation. My initial intent was to expose the fraudulent acts committed by the worker's compensation system, the insurance industry, the pharmaceutical companies, and the legal system. When I started writing this book, I was angry and hurt, determined to make a difference in the lives of people who suffered like us. In actuality, this book became a form of therapy that assisted in healing my own wounds. Putting our journey into writing now allows me to share the healing gifts I have been given as a result of my husband's injury, and provide you with tools to protect and take action on your own individual rights.

I believe that such gifts show up as challenges in life to teach us to be stronger, more independent, and more loving. It took me many years to learn to forgive and heal from these deep wounds—not physical wounds, but emotional attachments.

Also included are worksheets that provide questions for you to ask your doctor, attorney, and insurance company so you are aware of what is actually happening. There is a list of state resources for worker's compensation so you can contact them with questions about your specific state laws and learn how those will affect you.

The worker's compensation system, the insurance industry, the pharmaceutical companies, and the legal system have become so powerful that they are allowed to commit fraud and get away with it every year! The insurance industry ultimately controls all the options for healthcare in this country. The people who provide healthcare for us are responsible for practicing good faith; unfortunately, many of them do not. I suggest you learn what bad faith is and the top ten insurance companies cited by the insurance industry for bad faith practices.

This book would not be complete without a truthful explanation of our medical system. I am a healthcare provider. I will also share what happened to my husband, despite my having the connections and medical knowledge; I was unable to protect my husband and made many mistakes. *Please do not make those same mistakes.*

As a medical practitioner, a licensed nurse practitioner, and naturopathic doctor, I thought I understood the process and procedures my husband would undergo. I thought I could do proper research on what I didn't know and had the resources to find the information. I own an integrative medical clinic and it has been years since I performed services in a hospital setting, so knowing what happens inside that type of facility was new and different than what I practice every day.

I will explain the role your doctor plays in your worker's compensation claim and how managed healthcare affects your claim. I have outlined key advice for dealing with your doctors and the medical system. When taking on these large systems, crucial information is needed to fight this battle and win! This book also offers guidelines on finding the perfect attorney and what is needed to work with that person.

You need to understand exactly how problems occur over time with a claim. I have included my personal battle with the worker's compensation industry and the big medical conglomerates. Medical malpractice, worker's compensation fraud, insurance fraud, pharmaceutical fraud, and bad faith can happen to anyone!

Many of the areas in this book are controversial and most of the organizations and institutions mentioned here will not appreciate my exposing this information. Nevertheless, my intent is to be as objective as possible and to provide you with the tools you need to fight back.

I believe the primary motivation behind the corruption of the insurance industry, the medical community, and our legal system is money! Money can be a powerful incentive. Money and power are what make the world go round. It is my belief that the motivating factor behind the deception that occurred in my husband's situation was money! It destroyed a friendship and a man's career. It saved the insurance company over $100,000 in a medical claim, and provided a great side income for a doctor and his hospital. The motivation for committing fraud stemmed from power and money!

Insurance companies are publicly traded corporations; they have a legal responsibility to their shareholders to produce profits. There are very few companies that enter into business with the intent of losing money; most of them look for ways to increase profits. Companies have two ways to increase profits: sell at a higher price and produce at a lower price. Insurance and pharmaceutical companies are no different than other companies; they increase the premiums and pay out less by refusing coverage.

Do you remember what happened after Hurricane Katrina devastated New Orleans and the Gulf Coast in 2005? The storm and the flooding meant that millions of people lost their homes and belongings. Unfortunately, when they contacted their insurance carriers, they were told their plans did not have flood or natural disaster insurance, thus protecting insurance companies from having to pay out millions of dollars to the victims.

Have you tried to submit a claim to your medical insurance lately? Typically, claims are either delayed or denied the first time through. Insurance companies commonly use terms like "not medically neces-sary" or the claim is "considered experimental," or better yet, the claim is "not a covered benefit." My favorite insurance company excuse is, "We cannot process your claim until you provide us information on additional insurance coverage." If you have suffered an auto injury, I assure you they will expect you to submit the medical claims to an auto insurance company. Everyone seems to be passing the buck!

The courts have identified insurance as a business with a public interest. The industry no longer sees itself as a faithful servant of the people. With countless disputes in many areas, it has become the single largest user of the civil justice system. Later in this book, you will have specific information, along with the tools needed, to protect you and your family.

While I was conducting the research for this book, many people were afraid to come forward and speak up. They were concerned about the consequences and repercussions that might come from their insurance carriers, our healthcare system, and certainly how it might affect their livelihoods.

People often ask what one person can do. My husband said this to me many times throughout our ordeal. My answer was: "I can raise awareness, educate the public, and work to make a difference."

I started by contacting my senators and congressmen. I believed they would be concerned about the injustices happening every day to Americans. When the worker's compensation insurance company refused to pay for a second surgical procedure to remedy the impact of medical malpractice, I wrote my congressman. Surprisingly, the congressman's office contacted us to hear our story. However, shortly after hearing our story, we were informed he could not help us. We were not part of his district, but he would turn our concern over to the appropriate congressman. It was certainly no surprise when the congressman in our district never contacted us. I left messages with his staff several times without a response, but received nothing more than a generic letter thanking me for my concern.

If you believe our government is there to help us, the American people, I would suggest you think again. My experiences have led me to believe that everyone is looking out for himself or herself instead of doing what is right. Such behavior is what has prompted me to write this book, to turn an unfortunate situation into a more positive one. If our story can help you and others, then something good has come from our seven-year battle.

I felt it was important for people to know that if a medical practitioner can suffer from medical malpractice, it can happen to anyone. It is time to stop the nonsense! The American medical system needs reform. The driving force for performing medical procedures should not be to make money for hospitals and doctors. We need to stop taking advantage of human beings simply to cushion the bottom line for large healthcare conglomerates.

However, after writing the original account of our ordeal, I realized what I really needed was to find forgiveness. The only things that come from anger, hatred, and bitterness are more of the same. I was no longer willing to give my power away to the legal, pharmaceutical, and insurance industries. I realized I needed to return to my core belief and practice that I manifest everything in my life and that my life is a reflection of what I am feeling and who I am being.

As a result of this realization, I have become a more loving wife, mother, daughter, sister-in-law, and doctor. I have grown as an individual and learned to take a new place in the world of medicine. I am now grateful for this gift and thank God every day for the second chance.

Dennis, too, has grown from this experience. He lives every day like it might be his last, as he knows it. He enjoys the little things in life and has learned "not to sweat the small stuff." (We have included his thoughts and comments in italics.)

—Debra Muth

1. SEPTEMBER 11, 2006
CHANGED MY LIFE

September 11, 2006. The fifth anniversary of the attack on the United States. I would never have dreamed that a different type of attack would soon darken the doors of my family as well.

My family has worked very hard to have the house in the country, the cottage in the Wisconsin Northwoods, and all the toys that go with this lifestyle. My husband Dennis worked twelve-hour days at the factory and I was working and going to school, studying first to be a nurse practitioner, then to get my doctorate in Naturopathic Medicine.

We worked hard and struggled like most other Americans living the dream. We never counted on a single moment changing our entire life. I guess most people who experience a tragedy never realized how much their lives could change in a blink of an eye. It makes you recognize how precious life really is and what truly matters in this world.

That day started off like any other weekday, busy and productive, getting my kids—then eleven and fifteen—off to school, Dennis off to his job, and myself off to the medical clinic. We began the day with a moment of silence for those who had lost their lives and loved ones on September 11, 2001.

I had a busy day planned, with patients scheduled back to back and meetings at lunch. I was not expecting the phone call that would change my family's life forever. I remember it clearly: at 3 o-clock in the afternoon, the phone rang. It was my husband. This call was not unusual. He generally called in the afternoon before leaving for home just to check in on how our days were going and to say, "I love you."

This time the call was different. I could hear something in his voice that frightened me immediately.

"Hey, I hurt my back at work."

I immediately wanted to know the details. As a nurse practitioner, I began asking questions, anxiously listening to the symptoms, waiting to provide a diagnosis, and determine a plan of care. My mind flip-flopped between the role of practitioner and wife. Ultimately, I just wanted to make sure he was okay.

I could feel his distress over the phone.

As he described what had happened, I knew he was in trouble and began asking more questions.

"Was anyone with you?"

"Yeah!" he replied, "Mark and Don."

Dennis worked in a factory that made water meters. He started as a CNC operator and eventually after 15 years, worked his way to CNC maintenance mechanic.

He lifted heavy pieces of machinery every day, but on this particular day, he had unintentionally moved the wrong way. The pain was shocking and literally electrifying! The sharp jolt of pain that radiated down his back caused an explosion of heat to spread through his body. He started sweating profusely and was immobilized for a few minutes. This pain was unlike anything he had ever felt before!

Dennis worked with his brother Mark, who was the shop foreman, and Don, the shop manager and Dennis's good friend. The three men had worked side by side together for the past fifteen years.

On that particular day, the three men were deciding how to fix a turret lathe. A turret lathe is a large metalworking tool used to cut and shape pieces of metal. Dennis pulled on the 200-pound turret while Don and Mark stood by watching. There was a sudden movement and Dennis realized something was terribly wrong. The fear on his face was obvious to all around him. The pain was so intense that Dennis could barely speak.

Finally, he was able to utter, "Fuck, something is really wrong." He stood paralyzed for a few minutes. Then suddenly, he could feel his feet again and briefly wiggle his toes. When he tried to move his feet and toes, he could do so to a limited extent.. He still could not straighten up or stand erect.

The severe injury had been witnessed by a family member and a boss/friend, along with three other fellow factory workers. Mark and Don watched and made decisions regarding Dennis's medical care. One of those decisions should have been immediately taking him to the hospital for evaluation, but that was not what occurred.

Not all back injuries require immediate medical attention. But if a person cannot feel his/her legs, cannot move, or has nerve pain running down the legs, immediate medical attention is required.

Since Dennis could not move or feel his legs, the next move should have been taking him to Urgent Care for evaluation. Doing so protects the employer and the injured employee receives direct medical attention.

For people experiencing pain without serious signs of injury, use of ice applied to the affected area and taking anti-inflammatory medication such as Advil or natural anti-inflammatory herbs like boswellia can be helpful.

Somehow, when I got that call, my woman's intuition told me there was going to be a battle, and this incident was going to need a great deal of documentation. *Ladies, follow that intuition!* It will never steer you wrong.

The witnesses saw the look on Dennis's face when the electrifying pain shot down his legs and the mask of pain when he couldn't straighten up. Then they literally poured him into his manual-drive truck and told him to get home as soon as he could.

Don, his boss, told him, "In a few hours, you won't be able to move." Don assured Dennis that he had just pulled a muscle and would be fine. Dennis, frightened to his core, did what he was told. Using every ounce of strength to climb into that truck and get behind the wheel, he mentally prepared himself for the hour-long drive home during rush hour.

He later told me it took all his strength and determination to pump the clutch with a leg that didn't want to move. Excruciating pain rushed through his body. The pain increased with every movement. His diesel pick-up truck did not offer a smooth ride. Every bump in the road sent electrifying pain down his legs. All he could do is grit his teeth to bear agony in his back and into his legs. He prayed during the entire ride that he would just make it home and hopefully get some relief from the agonizing pain.

As he approached our driveway, he realized something was very wrong. He had just spent the past hour hunched over in his truck, pushing in a clutch, sweating, and grasping the steering wheel as tightly as he could. When he put the truck in "Park" and opened the door, he suddenly found he was unable to get out of the driver's seat. He couldn't move a muscle. He was paralyzed in that position. He honked the horn to get the attention of our two children so they could come down to the truck.

Kayla and Dillon had no idea why they were heading down to the truck. They thought their dad was bringing home something fun and wonderful. Imagine their shock when they found their father hunched over the wheel of his truck, unable to climb down from the cab without assistance! Our eleven-year-old son on one side and a fifteen-year-old daughter on the other carefully assisted their dad up twenty painful stairs to get into the house.

Every attempt to lift his legs shot excruciating pain from his spine down into his legs. Dennis was still covered in sweat. He was completely breathless when he reached the last stair—number twenty. What relief to have finally made it. Despite his own fear, he turned to his kids and apologized to them. He then reassured them that he was going to be fine.

That's when I received the second call from Dennis. His voice was shaking and he could barely speak as he gasped for air between words. He explained his inability to get out of his truck alone and attempt to climb the stairs; "I'm standing over the kitchen island. I can't walk any farther. The pain is so bad I can barely move."

Dennis then asked if I could bring home something for his pain. My fears were confirmed; if he was asking for pain medication, we were in trouble. He is a man who refuses to even use Tylenol. We are a holistic family, and I practice holistic medicine, so we avoid traditional medication whenever possible. I told him I would bring something home and would be there as soon as possible. He asked me to hurry. I knew he was frightened and in desperate need of relief.

After a brief consultation with my business partner, a medical doctor, we agreed that narcotics and antispasmodic (muscle relaxers) would be helpful. I left for home as quickly as possible. When I arrived after the never-ending 45-minute drive and rushed into the house, I could not believe my eyes. I found my husband sitting on the edge of a chair, holding his legs, hunched over, with a frightened look and sweat still pouring down his face. Fear coursed through me.

He said "I'm worried that something is really wrong."

Several hours had passed since the injury and the pain was raging out of control. Immediate medical attention had been withheld and driving home in a bouncing, manual-drive truck for an hour had aggravated his injury. I knew he needed medical attention.

Dennis refused to let me take him to the emergency room, for by that point, he could not bear the thought of another 35-minute drive anywhere. I conducted a brief medical exam and found that he was not able to bend over nor could he stand erect. Every movement caused severe pain that radiated down his legs.

Many times, if back injury patients can lie on a hard surface, they will begin to feel better. That was certainly not the case here. Once I got Dennis to the floor, which took several minutes, he began screaming in pain. He was incapable of straightening his legs or lying down. Sitting was definitely a bit more comfortable, but only with minimal move-ment. Dennis is fortunate to have a very high pain tolerance, but this injury was kicking his ass pretty hard. I knew this was not a muscle strain. What we were dealing with was something much worse.

I was finding it difficult to be both doctor and wife. Doctors should never treat their own family members because it is hard to be objective.

I was trying my best to not show my concerns, but I think Dennis was already fearful and knew something was not right.

Dennis doesn't trust conventional medical people. I was OK in his eyes, because I practice holistic and alternative medicine, in addition to being a nurse practitioner. Despite my urging, I was unable to convince him that he needed conventional medicine. He agreed to try the narcotics and muscle relaxants, and then we waited.

I gave him the medication and convinced him to try and lie on the couch. After he maneuvered his way onto the couch, he struggled with lying flat. He kept his legs bent, but tried to straighten them one at a time. It took about 30 minutes for the medication to take effect and he could finally relax. After several hours, I woke him and helped to the bedroom, as I thought that might be a better place for him to try to sleep. Once again, the pain medication allowed him to dose fitfully for a short while.

I sat by his side waiting as he lay in agony, praying he would be better by morning. We continued to administer regular doses of narcotics and muscle relaxants about every four to six hours, as instructed by my medical partner, for 18 hours straight.

The phone began to ring early that evening. The first call was from Mark, his brother, wondering how Dennis was doing. I answered his questions, but was concerned that whatever I said might get back to Don. The next call was from Dennis's parents. They, too, were concerned about what had happened and wondered how he was feeling. I began to explain that I thought the injury was more serious than a muscle strain. They, of course, were worried, but hopeful.

Later that evening, I even received a call from Don, Dennis's boss, supposedly out of complete concern for Dennis. Part of me did not trust Don; he was Dennis's boss and some of Don's past actions led me to my skepticism. Over the phone, Don provided me with a great deal of advice, because he also suffered from back trouble. I was told that Dennis should lie flat on a hard surface and apply ice. I informed Don that Dennis was unable to lie flat or on his side. The only things providing my husband any relief at this moment were the pain meds, which had put him into dreamland. Don insisted the back trouble would be over in a few days. I told him I would call to update him on Dennis's progress the next day, but not to expect Dennis to come to work.

That night was the first of many sleepless nights to come. Dennis was out of touch with reality after being dosed with pain meds, but still needed some relief. He tossed in bed the entire night, his legs moving uncontrollably back and forth, up and down, in excruciating pain. He was incapable of rolling over in bed and would grimace and groan with every movement, and even screamed out in pain in the middle of the night when he tried to move.

After a sleepless night, I knew he would need some additional medication, along with immediate medical attention. The morning stretched on forever, with Dennis lying in bed trying to find some comfort. He finally arose about noon that second day; the pain was unbearable.

On my way to work earlier that morning, I had immediately called Dennis's company to inform them that Dennis would not be into work that day. I had the pleasure of speaking with his brother, Mark, who normally handles these issues for employees. I began to describe the horrific pain Dennis had experienced during the night. I explained to Mark that Dennis definitely needed an MRI, and then began to ask questions about how this situation was going to be handled by the company. I assumed that a worker's compensation claim had already been filed, but my gut was telling me probably not. When I asked Mark directly about the claim, there was a hesitation, and then I finally heard "No."

This did not come as a shock to me, because I knew this particular company was famous for not filing worker's compensation claims when people got injured. Instead, it just paid off the employees and hoped the situation would go away.

Once again, I expressed my concerns about Dennis's condition, telling Mark, "This is much more than just a pulled muscle." Then I insisted the company file a claim. Mark told me he needed to speak with Don and they would get back to me. Within twenty minutes, I received the call telling me to file any medical claims directly to our personal insurance carrier. The company would reimburse us directly for any expenses or deductibles, but a worker's compensation claim would not be filed. I was also told Dennis's salary would be paid in full while he was off.

The Occupational Safety and Health Administration (OSHA) 29 CFR Parts 1904 and 1952 require employers to record and report injury and illness that is work related.

In Wisconsin, statute 102.31 requires employers to report injuries to their worker's compensation insurance carrier. Each state has different deadlines for reporting.

Dennis was very worried that my calling his employer would only cause trouble for him. At the time, he really believed he would be back to work in a day or two.

Now, being a naturopathic doctor, a nurse practitioner, and knowing the condition my husband was in, along with my experience with clients in similar situations, I was very uncomfortable. In addition, what I was being asked to do by Dennis's company was illegal. But this was not my employer nor was it my place to make any decisions to accept or decline this offer.

When I spoke with Dennis, he considered these requests appropriate because of the history he had with the employer. He really did not believe the situation was going to be so bad, nor that his boss would try to screw him—they were friends! I was not as confident. I did not trust the arrangement, but respected Dennis's decision, at least to a point.

My concerns arose from our history with the company. Dennis had been working there for fifteen years, and unfortunately, had seen many of his co-workers get injured on the job. They were paid for their time off, then terminated when they returned to work. One young man tragically cut off his hand in a machine; the company paid him his salary until he could return to work, then gave him a janitorial position for a few months before his position was eliminated.

SEPTEMBER 11, 2006 CHANGED MY LIFE

Dennis had also witnessed a loyal employee and friend of Don's who had been employed by the company for 20 or 25 years. When the man's wife became ill with cancer, and he began accessing the company-provided health insurance, his position was suddenly no longer needed and he was terminated without viable reasons. Dennis was worried he might be the company's next victim. Dennis felt he had everything and nothing to lose at this point. Little did he know that in actuality, it would be everything!

This situation would likely not have occurred if President Reagan had not decided that breaking up the labor unions in our country was a wise move. If my husband's shop had been unionized, this story would be very different. When an injury occurs at a union shop, there are procedures that must be followed and employees and their jobs are protected from unscrupulous employers.

Several years prior to my husband's injury, I was furious about the employee being terminated by the insurance company for his wife's cancer. So I called the Department of Health Services that governs HIPAA (the Health Insurance Portability and Accountability Act), a wonderful government-driven protection policy that is supposed to protect the rights of patients. I wanted to know what protection existed for workers employed by a self-funded insurance policy paid for by the employer.

Because I had healthcare experience and knew what questions to ask, I felt it was wrong to terminate an employee when his wife has cancer and they were using the insurance. In such instances, when employers are self-funded, they pay all the medical bills, so they are able to review any of the employees' medical conditions. Under HIPAA, a person's medical privacy is supposed to be protected. The reason for my call was that I knew of people being laid off after using the company's medical insurance. Unfortunately, the agency was only able to confirm that such action was definitely illegal, but could not help me prove it or stop this invasion of privacy.

What the hell! That is the agency that is supposed to protect the American people's health privacy; no one is supposed to be denied

HIPAA complaints can be filed by anyone who feels that their own or someone they know has had their personal healthcare information compromised by a qualifying agency. A qualifying agency is a medical provider, clearinghouse, or hospital.

Complaint Requirements:
- Must be filed in writing, either on paper or electronically, by mail, fax, or e-mail.
- Must include the name of the covered entity or business associate involved and describe the acts or omissions you believe violated the requirements of the Privacy, Security, or Breach Notification Rules
- Must be filed within 180 days of when you knew that the act or omission complained of occurred. (www.hhs.gov/ocr/privacy/hipaa/complaints) (Health and Human Services HIPAA, 2013)

insurance, fired, or not hired because of medical information. Not only are you protected from denials, NO ONE is supposed to be sharing such health information without release from the individuals concerned. If they do, a $10,000 fine and imprisonment are the result!

What good is this system if no one is there to enforce the rules? If the Department of Health and Human Services cannot or will not enforce the rules, then why report violations? This is the system we are up against!

Dennis was so angry; he could not believe that this organization was not willing to help. He has always been a little cynical about organizations supporting Americans and this just confirmed his belief that no one is willing to get involved or help the "little guy."

Our nightmare was only just beginning!

Dennis and I tried convincing ourselves that the horror stories we heard would never happen to us. We are honest people. Better yet, we thought we had a family member on our side, and the boss was Dennis's best friend; both men had witnessed the entire accident. Dennis and I truly believed things would be handled fairly. In all honesty, a little voice in the back of my head told me to be afraid, be very afraid! We wanted to trust his employer, give the company a chance, and Dennis really just wanted to go back to work.

2. THE RING OF FIRE

I knew Dennis needed medical attention, but I couldn't get him to the doctor because of my own packed schedule. And if I didn't just schedule an appointment, he would never agree to be treated. I arranged for an MRI (magnetic resonance imaging), a medical imaging technique used in radiology to visualize the internal structures of the body in detail. This is the best tool to use to see the nerves, muscles, and discs in the back—the very structures that needed to be evaluated.

Getting Dennis to the hospital proved quite challenging. He could not drive and my own day was full with patient appointments, so re-scheduling was not an option. My receptionist and friend offered to drive 35 minutes to my house to pick up Dennis and bring him back to town, then drive him to the hospital for his MRI, another 35-minute drive. She waited for him to have his test, drove him home, and then returned to work. It is fantastic to have friends and staff like Debbie Ellinger. Without her help that day, I do not know what I would have done.

Later I learned that during the MRI, Dennis had a very difficult time lying flat on the table to get the needed pictures. Lying flat was the worst position, not to mention having to lie still and straight for several minutes to get the images needed to make a proper diagnosis. Dennis had not been able to lie prone without moving since the incident. It was now September 12, 2006 and 24 hours since his injury. The MRI was scheduled in the early afternoon. He had only been awake a few hours and was being shipped off to the hospital, while still feeling the effects of the narcotics and muscle relaxers.

Anxiously awaiting the results, I did everything I could using my medical connections to rush the reading. It still took 24 hours of desperate waiting to get the results. The images confirmed my worst fear: a herniated disk and mild degenerative disk disease, along with a narrowing of the spinal canal, known as spinal stenosis.

A spinal disc herniation is a medical condition affecting the spine due to trauma, lifting injuries, or unknown causes, in which a tear in the outer, fibrous ring of an intervertebral disc allows the soft, central portion to bulge out beyond the damaged outer rings. Disc degeneration is a normal part of aging and for most people is not a problem, though for certain individuals, a degenerated disc can cause severe, constant, chronic pain.

Spinal stenosis is an abnormal narrowing of the spinal canal that may occur in any part of the spine. This narrowing causes a restriction to the spinal canal, resulting in a neurological deficit. Symptoms include pain, numbness, paraesthesia (tingling or pricking, feeling of needles), and loss of motor control. The location of the stenosis on the spine determines which area of the body is affected.

The diagnosis helped explain some of Dennis's symptoms. At least we knew what was going on. Not everyone who has a herniated disk suffers with long-term complications. That afternoon and in the following days, I spoke with many practitioners—chiropractors, orthopedic doctors, family practice doctors, and alternative medicine folks. Most said that a few weeks of rest and he should be back to normal. Little did we know what challenges the future would hold.

MEDICAL APPOINTMENTS GONE WILD

I was finally able to convince Dennis that he needed to see a doctor about his back pain four days after the injury. Dennis is not a fan of medical doctors, but also realized that he needed an objective evaluation, as well as documentation for the worker's compensation claim. Not wishing to put my MD business partner in the middle of what I sensed was going to be a mess, I had him refer Dennis to a neurosurgeon.

Being able to refer to colleagues and specialists is one advantage of being a nurse practitioner. Both Dennis and I were anxious to have the neurosurgeon confirm what we were seeing and explain the MRI in greater detail.

When we arrived at the facility, the receptionist told us we couldn't see the neurosurgeon because our insurance was out of network. I informed her that this was a worker's compensation claim and just because we were out of network did not mean we could not receive service. Amazingly, she really didn't understand what that meant.

Patients have an option to see a practitioner in or out of network. Receiving care "out of network" simple means that your insurance carrier will pay at a different rate, usually lower than paying the in-network rate.

Once we actually got to meet with the neurosurgeon, the consult lasted about three minutes. Two of those three minutes he spent looking at the MRI films, without ever even glancing our way. After a brief exam, and I mean brief—basically, the neurosurgeon checked Dennis's reflexes and palpated his back—we were told he had suffered a strain and was not a surgical candidate, so there was nothing the doctor could do.

Dennis and I looked at each other in dismay. The neurosurgeon neither offered pain medication—not even Ibuprofen—nor did he pre-

> **QUESTIONS TO ASK YOUR DOCTOR AFTER AN INJURY**
>
> - Do I need an MRI or CT?
> - Do I need an X-ray?
> - Should I undergo physical therapy?
> - Do I use heat or ice to assist in the discomfort?
> - Should I use Advil or Aleve? What dosage?
> - Should I limit my activities?
> - Do I have any lifting restrictions?
> - If there are work restrictions, get your healthcare provider to write them down for you.
> - Can I return to work? It is important for your healthcare practitioners to know what kind of work you do so they can give appropriate restrictions.
> - Can I drive?

scribe physical therapy. There was no discussion about work restrictions whatsoever! I had to bring up all these issues.

The neurosurgeon finally agreed to physical therapy and pain medication after I told him Dennis had been receiving these from his primary physician for the past week. He finally agreed to give Dennis five days off of work after we discussed the physical nature of his job.

It is my belief that this neurosurgeon was not interested in Dennis because "he was not a surgical candidate." This meant there was not a lot the neurosurgeon could do for him that would be financially beneficial to the doctor.

The brief visit with the neurosurgeon reinforced Dennis's belief that the pain must have been in his head. He looked at me after the appointment and said, "Maybe I should just go back to work."

This appointment was merely the beginning of the medical abuse we underwent. I am fearful of what would have transpired had Dennis attended this appointment alone, because he would have never known to ask for physical therapy, a medical work excuse, or pain medication. He would have believed that there was nothing wrong with him at all.

My advice: *never* let your injured loved ones go to appointments alone! If you are injured yourself, take someone with you. Do your homework

---

MORE QUESTIONS TO ASK YOUR DOCTOR

If you are being prescribed medication, ask what the drug is used for and what are the side effects you can expect.

- When can I expect the medication to begin to work?

- Can I expect a reduction in the pain or for it to completely resolve?

- How long can I expect to have pain?

- If the pain lasts longer than expected, will testing be ordered?

- Are there any symptoms I should be watching for that may indicate something else is wrong?

- When should I call the doctor or go to the emergency room?

- Where can I get more information about my condition that is reliable?

and speak up. I love it when patients come in to see me and come pre-pared with questions. If a doctor does not like that, too bad! Find one who listens and provides you with the answers you are seeking. This is your life and your health, and the health and well-being of your loved one! Remember, you are in control of your own life and your own destiny.

DECISIONS TO FILE THE WORKER'S COMPENSATION CLAIM

After five days of staying home, Dennis learned that his "generous" employer, who had earlier been so willing to pay for anything, was no longer willing to pay Dennis wages to sit at home with just a simple muscle strain. This "simple muscle strain" had left a rugged, strong, physically fit man unable to walk around the house without a walker for nine days. Nor was he able to take a shower by himself, or sleep in a comfortable position, or even get a entire night's sleep!

I began to investigate filing a potential worker's compensation claim at this time, researching on-line claims, rules, and regulations, and the consequences of not filing a claim. My digging sparked more questions and concerns about how things were being handled. I was convinced we needed to file a worker's compensation claim for Dennis's protection. Without a claim filed, a person can lose out on finan-cial and medical benefits.

Worker's compensation claims have prescribed time limits that need to be followed. Most states require that the injury be reported to the employer within 30 days of the injury. In some states, if the em-ployer knew about the injury, a claim can be filed anywhere from two to twelve years after the injury. By law, employers have seven days to notify their insurance carrier of the work-related injury, except in the case of fatality, which must be reported within 24 hours.

By law, worker's compensation insurance carriers must electroni-cally report all lost-time, compensable injury claims to the worker's compensation division within 14 days after the date of injury. The insurance company then has 30 days to report payment or dispute the claim. Each state may have different time frames for filing and pay-ment. I recommend that you check the laws in your particular state.

WORKER'S COMPENSATION REPORTING RULES

- All employers must report all work-related fatalities to the Worker's Compensation Division, within 24 hours.

- Insured employers must report any claim of an injury to their insurance carrier within 7 days.

- Self-insured employers and insurance carriers must report injuries that result in time lost from work four days or more after the date of injury to the Worker's Compensation Division.

- The report must be on a form WKC-12-E—First Report of Injury, or electronically filed, and must be filed within 14 days after the injury.

- Form WKC-13—Supplemental Report or its electronic equivalent must be filed by the 30th day after the injury or first day of lost time after the date of injury.

- Treating physician's medical reports for disabilities of more than 3 weeks as well as final payment reports for all reported claims are required.

- Employers are required to provide the Worker's Compensation Division, with OSHA survey information when requested.

Source: Department of Workforce Development, 2013

In those early days, Dennis still trusted his employer and was fearful about losing his job, so he really did not want to file anything that could jeopardize his job and livelihood. He was convinced that something must be wrong in his head, rather than in his body, because he had been told so by his boss, his brother, and even the neurosurgeon.

To make matters worse, like most American's these days, we were not in a financial position to be without his income. I felt that his employer was counting on the financial pressure to force Dennis to come back to work; we later found out that he had done the same to other employees in the past. In addition, we discovered that many insurance companies also figure that they can hold out longer than you can and drag their feet in submitting claims or making payments.

Dennis carried the family's health insurance, and of course, his income was needed to pay bills and buy groceries for our family. We lived on two incomes and were unable to see how we could rectify this right away. We needed to make some tough decisions quickly: either Dennis would go back to work and most likely incur additional injury, or we needed to find someone in the medical community who could help.

Looking back, my advice to you would be to change your lifestyle *today*. If your family is dependent on two incomes, reduce your spending as much as you can to be able to live on a single salary. Put the other salary into savings, even a health savings account. This will help you keep control of your destiny and reduce the possibility of living in fear and worry. In addition, make sure you have disability insurance, in case you are unable to work. Financially, you will be protected.

When you operate from a place of fear, you make decisions that you normally would not make. This fear is what every worker's compensation insurance carrier depends on. If you think you will not be able to pay the bills or feed the family, they win! They can hold out and you cannot. If you (or an injured loved one) returns to work before your healthcare provider clears you or you do not follow the medical recommendations, the worker's compensation insurance company can claim that you are not compliant, which is why you are not healing. This gives the insurance company a reason not to pay the claim.

For example, if your healthcare practitioner prescribes physical therapy three times a week, but you only go once a week, you are out of compliance and can be denied coverage. Some people do not attend therapy appointments as recommended due to financial constraints. Unfortunately, the insurance company does not have to pay for all these visits, but you will be held financially responsible. These appointments can become expensive and you will be required to pay them until the worker's compensation insurance company decides to reimburse these expenses.

When I started reading stories on-line about insurance companies and what they did to employees who were injured, I was appalled and shocked! I could not believe they would purposefully lose claims. Payments were delayed so the injured employee had to risk damaging his or her credit rating, or choose between medical care and mortgage payments.

This is the story I read that made me decide we needed to fight for what we believed in and what was right. It is presented by an attorney who worked on behalf of an unknown insurance company. I think it is extremely important to hear firsthand what is happening inside the insurance industry.

Confessions of a former insurance defense attorney

(By Sue Di Paola, Esq.)

Sometime around the early 1990s, the industry began to subtly, but radically change. First, there was a constant turnover in claims adjusters. There were fewer "career" adjusters and more clerks, generally young women, promoted within companies who were apparently set upon a path of training of which the emphasis was the denial of claims. Then another pattern sprung up. I found that if a claims examiner did not agree with defense counsel's legal advice, he or she would either try to get the lawyer to agree with them or pull the case, sending it to a lawyer who would agree to do what they wanted. Often, in attempting to formulate agreement, they would quote law as though the legal principles occurred in vacuum, rather than within the context of the facts of an individual case. Other times, they would purport to having obtained a "second opinion" from another lawyer so that they could argue about the case.

It became common for claims adjusters to allege that they did not receive reports and documents. Claims adjusters would then start to use phrases like "Let's starve them out!" or "This should drive them crazy!"

Thus, the philosophy "those with deeper pockets," meaning the insurance company or employer, can hold out longer than the injured employee. This certainly seemed to be the case for my husband and our journey. Employees had also heard my husband's boss saying similar things about our financial situation.

The new adjusters started taking these cases personally, so when employees hired an attorney, many adjusters became insulted. Adjusters would use phrases such as:

"If I don't pay, so what?"

"It's only a ten-percent penalty."

"Big deal!"

Penalties for delaying payments of claims meant nothing to these new claims adjusters. The attitude from the insurance companies was that they needed to send a message to the employee. The approach was to deny claims. Trying cases in court and appealing when the insurer lost, despite the fact that they knew full well that they would both lose, did not matter to the insurance carrier. These claims could end up being held up in court proceedings for many months and years. The employee's attorney's income was limited by state statute, therefore the attorneys would be waiting to receive payment as well. Adjusters would then state others would think twice before filing a claim!

As the business changed, my colleagues and I began to have closed door discussions about the ethical ramifications of following the directives of our clients. A serious dilemma was how to handle a client's outright rejection of legal advice, which would result in significant financial loss to the client. Any continuing education class on legal malpractice will teach an attorney to write a confirming letter to the client to docu-ment that the client has chosen not to follow it. To the insur-ance defense attorney, this is a confounding Catch-22. If such a letter is writ- ten, the result can be loss of business. However, without this documentation, we found that claims adjusters would willingly point the finger at the defense attor-ney for disastrous results, denying that the advice was given to them.

...Along with the increasing ignoring of legal advice, companies began to institute stringent fee guidelines and other "creative" arrangements to eliminate or reduce legal costs. In the mid- 1990s, many of my long-standing clients began to demand flat fees for handling of cases or sought to impose arbitrary fee guidelines. The result of this policy was that a client could very well insist that the attorney take the case to trial, but would "allow" only two hours for trial preparation. Since legal ethics, as well as maintaining our malpractice coverage, mandated that we prepare properly and thoroughly, the potential windfall savings for the companies were obvious. We could be exposed to suit if we didn't prepare properly. The other disquieting trend was the encouragement of bidding wars between attorneys, with the work going to the lowest bidder. This is a true conflict of interest to the detriment of the insured.

...In 1995, I was diagnosed with cancer. After a year of treatment and recovery time, I returned to work part-time. My own experience with a potentially terminal illness brought me face to face with the torment that persons who are injured or ill and decompensated are faced with when they cannot collect the benefits they paid for or are entitled to. After my own illness, I found it difficult to represent a client who would fight an injured worker for a disputed $30 medical bill. I would point out that the cost of my legal fees to fight would be higher than the disputed amount. However, all too often the client insisted on going to court and after losing, appealing the matter perhaps, many times in an effort to discourage injured or ill parties from pursuing claims. If the case was lost, the attorney would be blamed. If the case was won, "anyone" could have won it.

... When I retired some years later due to more surgery and serious disability I found myself wanting to make amends for being a dupe. I found myself facing the same nightmares o many of the claimant I met must have lived. Fortunately for me, the company I was dealing with, after "investigating" my claim for over a year, which included a "defense IME", agreed to provide the benefits I was legitimately due. I acknowledge, though, even though I was seriously ill, I still had a leg up on a "normal" claimant because of my unique experience.

...The more perplexing question is why adjusters working for public entities persist in unreasonable approaches to claims handling at the taxpayers' expense. I believe that it reflects a growing tendency of private insurers not to want to pay legitimate claims, which spills over perforce into claims handling in the public arena. Some attorneys have recognized this and realize that it is a serious personal, philosophical and moral dilemma. They have left the field and or crossed over to the other side and now represent claimants. I believe that companies have a right to be represented, but they do not have a right to require the representatives collude in questionable claims practices.

(*California Applicant's Attorney Association Journal*, June 2002)

Attorneys who work for the insurers depend on doing what the insurance companies and administrators tell them to do for their livelihood. These attorneys have children and families who in turn depend on them. Walking away from a paying client is not an easy decision. Many lawyers may not fully realize the consequences of what they are doing, but recognize that they could be fired for practicing ethically and fairly. Most attorneys just think that this will never happen to them.

A more interesting question is why the $10-an-hour insurance adjusters persist in unreasonable approaches to handling claims at the taxpayer's expense, forcing cases to court that should have never been sent to trial. To me, this situation appears to reflect a growing trend of private insurers not wanting to pay legitimate claims.

Be aware that claims adjusters will do anything to pay out as little as possible, even on a legitimate claim that involves serious injuries. These new insurance claims adjusters receive extensive training on how to save their companies money, but not necessarily how to properly examine and pay a fair settlement. Many insurance companies reward their employees for saving the company money by providing bonuses and promotions based on how much money they are able to save the company, rather than how many claims are settled. There are several ways for claims adjusters to accomplish this:

- **Using delay tactics**: Adjusters become masters at delaying their responses to claims and wearing people down. This is easier than you think. Most people will eventually give up calling, writing, or emailing, and the adjusters know this. Therefore, the injured worker will finally accept the insurance company's last offer just to be done with the whole thing.

  In Dennis's case, his employer delayed the claim by not filing on time and lying about how the injury occurred. Instead of admitting Dennis was injured at work, he claimed Dennis had been injured at home. The worker's compensation insurance carrier delayed by stating it had not received documents from our attorney.

- **Requesting unnecessary information**: Adjusters may repeatedly request documentation, even if the information does not have any relevance to the case or settlement. This tactic can easily frustrate people and again wear them down so they are more likely to accept a lower offer to just get things over with. I have heard many injured workers state that the insurance carrier requested medical records multiple times, claiming they never received the records from the patient's healthcare provider.

- **Disputing medical treatment**: Even though adjusters have had no medical training or knowledge, they are trained to dispute medical treatments recommended by your licensed physician. This will prevent you from receiving the appropriate medical care in a timely fashion, and result in a lower settlement for the insurance company.

  In Dennis's case, the worker's compensation insurance company claimed that Dennis was not injured at work and he did not need surgery. The claim was initially denied, and our medical insurance carrier was responsible for payment of all our medical expenses.

- **Nickel and diming**: Adjusters can try to only agree to pay a percentage of your past medical charges, again while having no medical background to make this decision. Adjustors know that most people will not hire a lawyer to challenge a small or seemingly insignificant portion of their medical bills. An example would be if you have $10,000 dollars in medical bills and the insurance adjuster offers you $6,000 dollars and does not offer you coverage for future medical expenses.

- **Telling you NOT to hire an attorney**: Insurance company adjusters will try to dissuade you from hiring an experienced attorney and falsely tell you that any money you receive will go to the attorney. Adjusters may even threaten to not pay a claim or low-ball a claim if you threaten to hire an attorney.

  Hire an attorney or at least talk with one if the worker's compensation insurance company threatens you or offers you a settlement that you feel is not appropriate.

- **Misrepresenting coverage**: Adjusters may misrepresent the amount of insurance coverage that is available to you. Worse yet, some insurance adjusters will not even inform you of the coverage or benefits available to you. This tactic may be used to entice you into accepting a smaller settlement, such as:

  - *Medical care*: Paid for by your employer to help you recover from an injury or illness caused by work

  - *Temporary disability benefits*: These are payments if you lose wages because your injury prevents you from doing your usual job while recovering.

  - *Permanent disability benefits*: Payments if you don't recover completely

  - *Supplemental job displacement benefits* (if your date of injury is in 2004 or later): Vouchers to help pay for retraining or skill enhancement if you don't recover completely and don't return to work for your employer

  - *Death benefits*: Payments to your spouse, children or other dependents if you die from a job injury or illness. This information can be found through your individual state

Department of Work Development. Each state has slightly different rules.

- **Acting as your friend**: There are times the adjuster will befriend you and make it appear that he or she is looking out for your best interests. These adjusters clearly are not! For instance, they may give you advice about medical treatment, then later decide not to pay for the treatment because the treatment was deemed excessive.

  At times, adjusters might tell you they have hired a medical case manager to assist you when you go to the doctor. They may also tell you they will send a nurse manager to assist you as well, so you understand all the medical information.

  Keep in mind you do not have to agree to this service and you certainly do not need to let this person into the exam room with you. Do not sign a release of medical information for them and tell your doctor that you do not want this person in the exam room with you. They can attend appointments but you do not have to discuss your medical case with them at all.

- **Making false promises**: There are times when adjusters may make promises to you that they knowingly cannot meet. For example, an adjuster may tell you that the insurance company will pay the in-jured person's medical bills until the person is recovered, then after a period of time, the insurer decides to not pay any longer, without informing the injured worker. Do not believe this when the adjuster tells you this. Adjusters cannot make agreements about paying for your lost time or medical bills without following the claims process.

These are only a few tactics used to wear down an already vulnerable person. It certainly doesn't seem right to take advantage of someone when he or she is already down, but I'm sure it happens all the time.

For some attorneys and claims adjusters, the worker's compensation insurance game has led to serious personal and moral dilemmas. Some have left the field and others have become advocates for injured workers. I personally believe that both sides—the insurance companies and the injured workers—deserve legal representation. However, I also feel that both sides should play by the rules and be fair.

Myths about Worker's Compensation Claims in Tennessee
Keith Williams Law Group
(excerpted from http://www.keithwilliamslawgroup.com/library/common-myths-about-workers-compensation-claims-in-tennessee.cfm

The workers compensation insurance company adjuster's job is to do the right thing. Never forget that what constitutes "the right thing" is a matter of perspective. What you and I think is the right thing (paying you the full amount to which you are entitled) is not necessarily what a workers compensation insurance company thinks is the right thing. Worker's Compensation insurance companies are in business, after all, to make a profit.

You have to give your employer's workers compensation insurance company a recorded statement before consulting with an attorney or they won't pay your temporary workers compensation benefit payments. Every word in your statement you give them about what happened can be used against you in order to try and minimize liability of your employer and their insurance company.

If you submit a reasonable settlement demand to the workers compensation insurance company, you will get a reasonable settlement offer in return. The insurance company wants to pay out as little as possible on every claim. Insurance companies establish their range of settlement authority in a case based on what they perceive as their potential exposure.

You can recover for pain and suffering in a Worker's Compensation claim. You cannot recover money for pain and suffering in a Worker's Compensation claim.

Your workers compensation claim will be decided by a jury. Ninety-nine percent (99%) of worker's compensation cases settle without a trial.

All worker's compensation lawyers have the same training and certifications. Not all attorneys have the same training and certifications. Different areas of the law involve different legal knowledge, skills, and areas of practice.

Taking advantage of anyone who has worked for an employer, who was injured on the job, and is now struggling to keep family, home, and livelihood intact, just seems unfair.

I was furious by the time I read the attorney's article and had done more research on the whole insurance field. How could this be allowed in our country? Could the corruption so many talk about be true? If this was the case, then Dennis needed to fight to protect not only his health, but also everything he has worked for in his life like never before.

3. ADVOCATING FOR OURSELVES

Dennis's last day of medical leave was quickly approaching and his decision to file a claim—or not—could not be put off any longer. We had a tough choice: should he return to work or go back to the doctor for more evaluations? I knew he couldn't return to work and lift 200-pound parts again. I contacted his neurosurgeon and explained Dennis's lack of progress, his severe pain, and his inability to walk without a walker or shower without assistance. I further described Dennis's inability to bend over at the waist. Performing normal, daily activities caused excruciating pain. I questioned how Dennis could return to his job without restrictions and thought he needed further evaluation.

Prior to his injury, Dennis worked as a maintenance man for a machining company. Dennis's job was fixing large computerized machines called CNC, a machine tool that uses programs to automatically execute a series of machining operations via a computer. Along with this, Dennis performed building maintenance that required repeated heavy lifting, crawling, and squatting throughout an entire 12-hour shift. How could he return to this type of work without being able to bend and more importantly, without injuring himself more? That was the ultimate question.

I was concerned that the neurosurgeon would not understand my worries, since he had only met us for a three-minute consultation and had not even conducted a complete exam.

Fortunately, the neurosurgeon agreed to provide Dennis with limited light-duty work restriction for two weeks. He then referred us to a pain management specialist, as well as referring us back to our family practice doctor.

Imagine our surprise when Dennis returned to work a few weeks after the injury, his job had already been given away, not just to another employee in the company but to a new person who had been hired to replace him. Dennis was told the company could not survive two weeks without a maintenance man. It was at that moment the picture became very clear to Dennis. The friendship and the family connection meant nothing. Dennis was suddenly no different than any of the other injured workers who had preceded him at that company. He was a liability to the company, rather than a valued friend and co-worker.

Dennis needed to begin thinking more clearly and play defense, instead of letting fear run his decision-making ability. It was already too late. He knew the truth: his job was already gone and there would be no job once his doctor released him. If he didn't start watching out for himself, he would be doomed. It was never his intention to get an attorney. Of course, we had discussed doing so, but Dennis could not have imagined suing his supposed friend, but now it was war!

Dennis called me that morning to tell me what just happened. He began the conversation with "They hired someone else for my job."

My response was a stunned, "What?!"

He followed up by telling me that all the guys were treating him strangely. "They won't talk to me or look at me. Don would not come near me." These were people Dennis had worked with for over 15 years.

What finally convinced Dennis to seek legal counsel was a few hours after he arrived at work, he decided to confront his brother. Dennis asked Mark point-blank, "What's happening with my job?" I think Dennis really needed to hear the truth. He was living in a world of fear, but also one of unrealistic beliefs. He did not want this to be happening to him. He did not want his brother to turn on him, or his friend to treat him the way he had treated other workers before him. I think the hardest thing for Dennis was to hear Mark confirm that his job was really gone.

We both instantly knew something was wrong. I then spent a good portion of the morning contacting several attorneys to discuss his case.

They all directed me to one of the best in the business. I made the call and discussed our situation with the attorney. I told Dennis if he was interested in getting legal counsel, all he needed to do was call that lawyer.

Dennis shrugged me off and said "I don't want to do that to Don. He's my friend. I taught him to ride a motorcycle. We snowmobile together." I reminded him of how he was being treated now. Out of nowhere, Dennis then asked me for the attorney's number and told me he would call me later. I was shocked because such rapid action was completely out of character for my husband.

That afternoon, Dennis told me he had spoken with the attorney, who would later become his attorney. Dennis shared his story, the entire story, including the part about the other men who were let go. The attorney began to explain to Dennis what rights he had as an injured employee. He told Dennis he had seen this happen to many people before and had dedicated his life to helping injured employees. The attorney suggested to Dennis that if he wanted to protect himself, he should exercise his right to medical therapy and leave work. After that, Dennis should drive directly to the law office and start a claim.

Dennis was still not convinced that legal action was the right route to take. He told the attorney he would think about it and thanked him for the information. After a few hours at work that first day, the conversation with Mark and the treatment of his coworkers, Dennis knew immediately what had to be done. No longer feeling fearful, he pulled the doctor's note from his pocket and threw it at his boss—no longer his brother! Dennis walked out of the shop and went to his truck, grasped the handle, and pulled himself up into the truck with pain and aggravation. Without hesitation, he drove to the lawyer's office and met with the attorney. That was the only choice he had if he was going to protect himself and everything he worked so hard to build during his life. It all came down to that one moment!

Dennis was angry and fearful. His worst fear was coming true. He had become like the other employees before him who had been injured. He could not believe his friend and his brother both turned on him.

When I later spoke with the attorney, he told me that was pretty standard behavior for injured workers. Fear can cause them to make decisions that are not necessarily in their best interest. People fear the loss of their jobs, their work friendships, and what will they do financially.

Dennis and I thought this would be the answer to our prayers. After all, once his employer was forced to file the worker's compensation claim, everything would be fine. We would be protected! Since 1914, the worker's compensation system has been protecting employees from losing all they have worked for their entire lives, including their jobs. Why should it be any different now?

WHAT REALLY HAPPENS

We were about to receive a free education about the real world of worker's compensation, employers, doctors, and attorneys. Unfortunately, the real eye-opener for Dennis and me was that none of the players in this game play fair. They have their own agendas, and they play to win. If you are going to play this game, you need to play to win as well!

THE DOCTORS / THE MEDICAL SYSTEM

My husband started out receiving care in the medical system, as do all other injured people. I am sure there were a few doctors along the way who thought he was faking his injury, so they did not provide adequate care. Dennis is a man who never claimed an injury in over 22 years. He had never suffered a back injury before and had never missed work. We are good, upstanding citizens. Why would we lie about his being injured?

I realize now that these doctors did not know any of this about us. They honestly did not believe Dennis's injury was as bad as it appeared.

I am a nurse practitioner with a doctorate in naturopathy. As practitioners, we all make mistakes and we all misjudge patients. This makes us human and open to errors—we can never forget that.

The neurosurgeon decided it was time for us to see the pain management specialist, as well as a physiatrist. Physiatrists, also known as rehabilitation physicians, are nerve, muscle, and bone experts who treat injuries or illnesses that affect movement.

The pain management specialist was wonderful. She spent time with us and explained all available options to attempt to relieve pain. The specialist began her physical exam, then looked at me and said, "He doesn't have any reflexes."

I was so relieved. No one we had visited to that point would confirm what I knew. She suggested that Dennis undergo spinal epidural injections (steroid injections). An epidural steroid injection delivers steroids directly into the epidural space in the spine. Needless to say, these injections are incredibly painful. Dennis underwent three injections over a few weeks but these only provided minimal pain relief for 48 hours. We quickly decided to abandon this treatment option, since a person is only supposed to receive three steroid injections in a year. Let me say this again: *only three cortisone or steroid injections in one year.*

Steroid Injections

Steroid injections have been used to treat low back problems since 1952 and are an integral part of the non-surgical management of sciatica and low back pain. The goal of the injection is pain relief; at times, the injection alone is sufficient to provide relief. Although many studies document the short-term benefits of epidural steroid injections, the data on their long-term effectiveness are less convincing. More studies are needed to properly define the role of epidural steroid injections in low back pain and in sciatica. Despite this, most studies report that more than fifty percent of patients find measurable pain relief with epidural steroid injections. The pain relief can vary between patients lasting anywhere between one week and one year.
Source: Richard A. Staehler, 2007

I see many people in my practice who have undergone five or more of these in a year. This puts your body at serious risk for bone loss, so do not allow anyone to do this to you.

The next doctor to assist with the pain was a physiatrist. Unfortunately, this turned out to be a waste of time. We chose a doctor who was trained in acupuncture. Dennis and I both believe in complementary therapy and felt she would be open to a more integrative approach, since the herniated disk was inoperable according to the neurosurgeon.

To our disappointment, this doctor refused to provide acupuncture or any other integrative therapy. This physician offered ibuprofen at the first visit, which might have been be fine if Dennis had not already been through steroid injections and narcotics without relief.

During the visit, we were told the MRI never showed a herniated disk and that the injury was only a muscle strain. I explained that a muscle strain does not require cortisone injections and usually responds to Valium and Oxycodone; neither medication had done anything to relieve Dennis's pain. I also pointed out that a muscle strain does not cause decreased reflexes and a limp. I also questioned the actual commentary in the report that specifically states that Dennis had a herniated disk. She told us she had not seen that.

Had she even read the report? I had and knew exactly what it said! She thought an antidepressant with an additional anti-inflammatory agent would be helpful. Imagine my fury!

Do patients have to act as their own doctors? It certainly seems like it, at least in some situations. It's bad enough that patients are injured, suffer with pain and other debilitation, as well as having to rearrange their family and work schedules. Patients are also busy trying to adjust their financial lives so that they do not lose everything they worked so hard to build.

When are Americans, consumers, and humans, going to stop this tyranny? When will we stand up and say enough is enough? It is my belief that it is our personal responsibility to stand up for what is right and protect our loved ones.

I thought Dennis and I were doing everything possible to find a solution to his pain. Being a healthcare professional myself, my ego told me I was smarter and that I had some inside information about particular doctors, so I could pick the best of the best. With the right information, we could avoid the healthcare problems and make good decisions. I thought I was asking all the right questions.

Let me tell you, that could not have been further from the truth. I had an instant lesson in the medical world from the patient's side, along with my naivety about worker's compensation. Who would have thought that the medical world I knew was so different than the one I was about to enter. I needed to learn quickly about so many things. I did the only thing I knew how—I began researching all the information I could about doctors, surgeons, herniated disks, and treatment options.

You may be wondering why a doctor would have to do research. You might think that I should know all about such conditions. Most doctors specialize in various areas. I am a nurse practitioner and naturopathic doctor; my specialties are women's health and natural medicine. I know the basics about back pain and injuries, but not surgery. I am a novice in this arena, just like every other back injury patient.

If you are going to advocate for yourself, you need to have the knowledge to ask appropriate questions. Do not be afraid to ask questions and share your concerns with the doctors or practitioners with whom you are going to work.

SURGICAL EVALUATION

It took several long months to complete the research that led us to a surgeon who was highly recommended and had a good reputation. As a matter of fact, my office had made referrals to him in the past and we never heard anything but wonderful things about him. The first visit was amazing. He spent an hour with us! Yes, a whole hour!

These days, it's almost unheard of for doctors to spend so much time with a patient. This doctor was thorough with his exam, and spent a great deal of time explaining what he thought was happening. We finally had an answer to why Dennis had been suffering in pain for the

Normal and slipped disc. Artwork showing a normal (top) and slipped (bottom) disc in the backbone, seen from above. The rear of the backbone (with protruding processes), and the spinal cord and spinal nerves are at bottom in each view. The intervertebral discs are located between and cushion the vertebrae (white), the blocks of bone that form the backbone. When one of these discs ruptures, the fluid and displaced tissue can put pressure on the nearby nerves, causing pain. The condition usually gets better with rest, but severe cases may need surgery. (ScienceSource 2014)

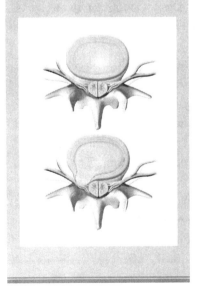

past six months. We were so relieved someone believed that Dennis wasn't faking!

Now Dennis could finally get the medical care he needed and heal. The surgeon was able to explain to us that when Dennis twisted and lifted at the same time, it was like twisting the top off of an Oreo cookie. The doctor even brought out an Oreo and removed the top by twisting. The white cream inside doesn't come off evenly, and causes what is called an annular tear. To prove this, a procedure called a Discogram would have to be performed. This procedure is incredibly uncomfortable, but would prove the doctor's theory. Dennis was eager to get this done. He just wanted to get better.

Six months had already passed and Dennis's pain was worsening. Spring was on its way and Dennis is a big spring turkey hunter. It would also be the first year that our youngest son could go turkey hunting, and Dennis didn't want to miss that for anything! The day of the Discogram brought with it a great deal of stress, but as usual, Dennis was upbeat and had a great attitude.

Neither of us realized exactly how difficult the test would be. The test involves placing needles into the spine, then blowing air and dye into the disc space. No anesthesia or pain medication is used; one can only imagine the pain. Picture a man lying on his stomach without pain meds, and add to it the tension and stress of waiting for the needle to be put in your spine. Nothing could prepare you for the pain involved when air is blown into the space. The test is positive if it reproduces the normal degree of pain felt with the injury. Fortunately, Discograms are generally over within a matter of 30 minutes and usually, only three or four needles are stuck into the spine. Dennis had *eight*—eight needles pushed into his spine with air blown into each one!

The doctor was not able to get proper placement due to Dennis's spinal stenosis, the narrowing of the spinal column that causes pressure on the spinal cord. Dennis tried everything he could not to scream during this procedure. When it was finally over, he came out and said never again!

Thank goodness, this painful procedure produced the information needed to prove what the surgeon suspected, but Dennis's pain was even more severe for days afterward.

We patiently waited for the results, wondering what was going to happen, how bad the injury was, and how we were going to continue to pay for all of the treatment and medical care. At our appointment, the surgeon reviewed the results of the Discogram, which confirmed his initial diagnoses a grade-5 annular tear. In layman's terms, what our surgeon was describing was a broken back.

He proceeded to tell us the only option we had at this point was to undergo a surgical procedure called a fusion. A fusion is a surgical technique in which one or more of the vertebrae of the spine are united together ("fused") so that motion no longer occurs between them. It can take several months before the vertebrae are actually fused together.

There are many possible reasons for a surgeon to consider fusing the vertebrae. These include: treatment of a fractured (broken) vertebra; correction of deformity (spinal curves or slippages); elimination of pain from painful motion; treatment of instability; and treatment of some cervical disc herniations. A person should not make the decision about disc fusion lightly; it can affect his or her life forever.

Recovery following fusion surgery is generally longer than for other types of spinal surgery. Patients usually stay in the hospital for three or four days, but a longer stay after more extensive surgery is not uncommon. A short stay in a rehabilitation unit after release from the hospital is often recommended for patients who had extensive surgery, or for elderly or debilitated patients.

The fusion process varies in each patient as the body heals and incorporates the bone graft to solidly fuse the vertebrae together. The healing process after fusion surgery is very similar to that after a bone fracture. Substantial bone healing does not usually take place until three or four months after surgery. In addition, smokers have a longer recovery process because it decreases the oxygen supply to the new tissue.

There was a brief discussion regarding the type of bone graft that would be used during the surgical procedure and we were sent off to schedule our procedure with the support staff in his office.

4. THE HISTORY AND TRUTH BEHIND WORKER'S COMPENSATION

The American worker's compensation program began in the early 1900s. It was started to protect companies and provide workers with an automatic recourse when injured or hurt on the job. Before such a worker's compensation program, injured workers were forced to sue their employers for lost wages and medical expenses. This resulted in lost jobs and hefty settlements that exceeded what was necessary on a case-by-case basis.

After Dennis's and my experiences, I am guessing it was implemented to protect the business, not the employee.

Historically, worker's compensation developed from the English law of "vicarious liability" established in the 1700s. This law made a master or employer liable for the negligent acts of a servant or employee. In 1837, an English case modified vicarious liability so that the law no longer held the employer liable if the employee or servant was found negligent for an injury to himself or herself or a co-worker. This doctrine of assumption of the risk presumed that employees could refuse dangerous job assignments, relieving the employer of liability when those jobs caused injury or death. Employers could now use the defense of negligence that completely absolved them of liability. (Guyton, 1999)

Workers were left with inadequate resolutions against their employers for injuries resulting from work. Industrialism was expanding and there was an increase in work injuries. By the end of the nineteenth century, countries were recognizing that there was a problem and began to look at compensation systems.

In 1884, Germany had developed a system where the employer and employee shared in the cost of subsidizing workers who became disabled by injury, illness, or old age. In 1897, England developed a similar system called the British Compensation Act. This movement reached the United States after the Civil War. (Guyton, 1999)

In the United States, various state representatives met in Chicago in 1910 to draft a uniform worker's compensation Act that was finally enacted at the national level in 1911. Wisconsin was the first state to adopt the law. By 1920, every state had some type of worker's compensation insurance, which is essentially a pact between the employer and employee. It is an employer-mandated program to cover medical care and replace wages for injured workers, along with certain other expenses.

Worker's compensation is different than any other type of insurance because it is based on no fault or negligence. The idea behind worker's compensation is not to punish an employee, but rather to protect employers from lawsuits and injured workers from destitution. The ultimate goal of this type of insurance is to return injured employees to work without harming the employer's business.

By law, every state is required to have some type of worker's compensation program. However, the laws may vary amongst jurisdictions. An employee who sustains personal injury as a result of the employment is automatically entitled to certain benefits. Benefits include lost wages, payment of medical treatment, provision of vocational rehabilitation or job replacement assistance, and in the case of a work-related death, benefits are passed onto the employee's dependents. Independent contractors are excluded from worker's compensation protection.

Some of the benefits covered by worker's compensation insurance include retraining or rehabilitation. There are limits to the payout depending on the type of injury and the body part that is injured. This will also depend on the state that you live in. This information can be found on state websites.

Without worker's compensation, two options are available to the injured worker. A company could decline assistance and force the worker to fund his own medical care and unemployment, which could leave the injured worker destitute. There could be government assistance such as Medicaid, welfare, or food stamps. This could help an injured worker survive, but at the expense of the local taxpayers.

With a worker's compensation program in existence, the injured worker receives an income and payment for medical care from a private source, instead of a governmental program or at the taxpayer's expense. It is not the goal of the worker's compensation system to punish the employer, so states require employers to establish a self-insured fund or to buy a worker's compensation insurance policy. Essentially, employers pass on the costs of worker's compensation benefits or insurance premiums in the pricing of their products. Therefore, consumers are ultimately the ones who fund the worker's compensation system.

Not everyone is in favor of the current worker's compensation program in the United States. There are laws that provide incentives to larger corporations to move their production to areas where compensation laws do not exist or are far less expensive. (NAIC, 2006). Small businesses also complain that the premiums are too high and place a burden on their operations.

In exchange for submitting a worker's compensation claim, an injured worker loses the right to sue the employer. However, the injured worker does have the right to sue a third party whose negligence caused or contributed to the worker's injury, even if he or she receives worker's compensation.

An example of this would be a worker who is driving somewhere for the company and is in an accident at the fault of someone else. The injured worker is covered by worker's compensation, but can additionally sue the other motorist under a common law theory. If the worker recovers money from the negligent motorist, the worker must repay the employer or insurer-paying worker's compensation benefits; he or she can keep what is left. In some states, the employer or insurer paying worker's compensation benefits may sue a negligent third party on behalf of an injured worker in hopes of recovering part or all of the benefits.

From an insurer's point of view, denying coverage for large claims has become an effective and possibly even a necessary strategy. Insurance companies have financial incentives to not pay a claim immediately. From a policyholder's view, the efforts and cost of collecting a claim have gone up and the reliability of insurance has gone down.

It can become a nightmare for injured employees when employers choose not to carry worker's compensation insurance because the premiums are deemed too expensive. For example, a loyal employee twists his knee at work and it gives out. He tells the boss, who tells him to put ice on it and rest. Several days later, the knee is swollen and painful. He is told by the employer to go have it checked out. A trip to the doctor involves x-rays, a brace, and pain medication, not to mention that the worker is taken out of the work environment for a short period of time. The employee is not concerned because he believes the bills will be paid and his income will not be interrupted because worker's compensation is mandatory.

Weeks go by. The worker does not receive a call to approve further testing and he begins to hear that there are insurance problems. He starts to call the employer and is told to claim it on his personal insurance. Red flags go up. Later, the worker finds that there had been a lapse in the worker's compensation premium payments, with the excuse that the payment was sent to the wrong address or it was lost in the insurance system.

Soon the company is calling the worker and accusing him of telling stories to get the employer in trouble. Then the ugly truth comes out; the company never had worker's compensation insurance and is now complaining that it has been fined and the medical costs have put it out of business. The worker is left on his or her own.

The worker then contacts the employment office and is told that since he was injured on the job, he does not qualify for unemployment benefits. He is then directed to contact the labor board and an attorney. He again is told there is nothing they can do except look into the situation. The worker's medical bills are increasing, he is falling further behind in his bills, has no insurance, no job, no food, and he is in pain.

He then hires an attorney and gets advice to apply for state medical aid so he can get necessary medical treatment. The attorney contacts the company, which states that it disagrees with the injury. The company claims the injury occurred elsewhere and refuses to pay any bills.

This scenario is too close to home for Dennis's situation. The difference for us is that my husband's employer did have worker's compensation insurance, but chose not to submit the claim to the insurance company to save the business money.

This should scare you. It did us! The last thing you need is to find yourself in this situation! Do everything you can to protect yourself. Check out your employer. If your employer has worker's compensation insurance, check out its track record on payment and claims. This should be public knowledge, but might be difficult to find. Start with your state's insurance commissioner. The Internet is another great place to do some preliminary research.

Some people believe that privatization of worker's compensation insurance is the answer. West Virginia is the latest state to move from a state-funded program to a privately funded host of competitive companies. Privatization never comes without risks and controversy.

Whether public or private, worker's compensation remains a significantly controversial topic in the United States. I suspect it will remain that way for many years to come. There is no safe program that protects all, but there has to be a system that is better than what we currently have. Today, insurance companies have the upper hand and the hard-working employee is the one who gets left holding the bag.

Once an employee is injured on the job, there are several applicable laws to protect both the employee and the employer, or better yet, the insurance company. First, in order for an injury to be deemed viable for "worker's compensation," the injury must occur on the job. The definition of "during employment" means that the injury occurred during the time you were actually on the clock with your employer. A few examples: you are driving to the bank to make a deposit for your company and someone runs a red light and hits your vehicle; this would be considered a "worker's comp" injury. You are at work, bend over to pick up a box and injure your back; this is a "worker's comp" injury. You are repeatedly exposed to chemicals suspected of causing disease and after twenty years of daily exposure to the chemicals you develop lung cancer; this is a "worker's comp" injury.

WORKER'S COMPENSATION
FROM THE EMPLOYER'S PERSPECTIVE

According to Tsuneishi Insurance Agency, "Insurance companies don't pay for your employee's injuries; they just finance them for you at higher interest rates!" Employers pay $2 to $3 to the worker's compensation insurance company for every dollar they pay out for an employee's injuries. Employers have worker's compensation insurance because the law requires it. Having worker's compensation insurance "spreads the true cost of the employee injuries out over time," according to the same source.

Each claim results in an extremely expensive financing contract. Employers pay premiums and then have to pay for almost all of the worker's claims. Actual and intangible costs to the employer include:

- Payment from worker injuries through lost dividends and return of premium

- Lost productivity

- Reduced morale for the unhurt workers who fill in for the injured worker

- Increased stress for management and staff

Because employers are aware that they are ultimately paying for a worker's injuries, it is critical that the employer demand aggressive claims management. Employers cannot just notify the insurance company about an injured worker and expect the insurance company to "do its job." Employers should oversee the management of the employee's case. It behooves the employer to have the injured employee heal quickly so he/she can return to work. The cost of replacing qualified employees is very high to the employer. Returning good employees to the job quickly is beneficial to the employer.

It is ultimately the worker's compensation insurance carrier that manages the claims and controls when and how much is paid out to cover the expenses of the injured employee.

Every business or company should have an employment policy in place that defines the exact process to follow when a worker becomes injured, even if that injury is a minor cut that requires a small Band-Aid. Having a process in place protects not only the business owner, but the worker as well.

Dennis's employer did not have a policy in place prior to my husband's injury. It was Dennis's case that encouraged the business owner to put such a policy in place to protect the company and other employees in the future. We are happy to see that now when someone gets hurt at the firm, he or she is taken to the doctor immediately for evaluation and medical attention.

Worker's compensation insurance premiums are based on several factors, such as location of the business, the number of claims filed each year, the amount paid out in injury claims annually, the business owner's and manager's experience, and the type of work such as clerical vs. high-risk construction work. These costs also depend on coverage limits, endorsements, deductibles, and the overall claims history of that class of business with the chosen insurance company.

CompMonitor is a unique system that reviews and audits individual claims for employers to assure the claim is being valued correctly and is closed appropriately instead of being dragged out and costing the employer more money. According to CompMonitor, there are six things companies can do to lower insurance costs and protect their workers from injury:

- Implement programs to reduce injuries and their costs.
- Develop or refresh a safety program.

- Provide worker training.

- Identify workers having multiple worker's compensation claims.

- Institute a safety incentive program.

- Initiate a supervisor safety awareness program and monitor this program.

Why would an employer dispute a worker's compensation claim? The answer is simple and boils down to a single, five-letter word: *money*. Employers pay worker's compensation premiums based on the type of work and number of employees. It is also possible that employers under -report earnings to reduce the worker's compensation reimbursement rate. There can be a misclassification of payroll, for example, when an employer reports that a roofer is actually performing duties for a clerical position. (DeCarlo, 2009)

RECOMMENDATIONS

It is important to notify your employer immediately upon discovery of your injury and give specific details regarding how it occurred. Make sure you include the names of any witnesses who know of the injury. Usually the employer requires a form to be completed with the details of the injury, along with your signature and the employer's. Depending on your injury, your employer may require a medical evaluation shortly after the injury to confirm the details of the injury.

Once your medical practitioner evaluates you, inform your employer about the results. If you are being told to take off from work, you will need to have written documentation to provide to your employer. Usually this is completed by your healthcare practitioner in the form of a prescription with your restrictions, or your employer may have specific paperwork to be completed and returned to the company.

Medical expenses that relate to your injury will be billed to the worker's compensation insurance company. If it does not pay for your medical expenses, your private insurance is then billed. The private medical insurance company has the option of denying payment; then you are left responsible for any medical bills until your worker's compensation claim is settled. You may also be required to pay for treatments up front and then get reimbursed by worker's compensation insurance.

Payments are made weekly to the employee by the insurance company once the claim has been proven to be work-related. Checks do not always arrive to your doorstep on a weekly basis. Sometimes they can be delayed. You could have several case workers assigned to your case over a year or two; many of them either quit or are replaced for various reasons.

In our case, we received two or three checks at a time, and then several weeks or months would pass without a check. No one at the insurance agency has an explanation for why the checks are delayed; that is just how the system is.

If you have hired an attorney, he or she cannot offer much help either. The attorney can call the insurance company or send a letter, but there is no guarantee that your check will arrive any sooner. I called our attorney when the checks were three or more weeks behind, and he would send a letter to the insurance companies' attorney. Shortly after that, we would receive payment again, at least for a while and then back to normal.

Words of wisdom: you will have to be patient and diligent with your case. Document everything and get copies of everything, including the report filed by your employer. Also, learn and understand all you can about the system and your case will help a great deal.

BEING PAID BY WORKER'S COMPENSATION INSURANCE

Worker's compensation insurance provides financial reimbursement for lost wages and medical benefits to a worker who has sustained an injury as a result of an accident or occupational disease on the job. The worker receives financial support, usually on a weekly or biweekly basis, to compensate for lost wages. In addition, medical benefits are paid out. The question of negligence or fault is not supposed to be an issue, but as you have read, the worker's integrity may come into question.

Worker's compensation benefits are typically paid at 66 percent, or two-thirds, of a worker's regular wages or salary. This is usually a gross dollar amount. Ordinarily, workers compensation benefits are not taxable, but you should check with your state worker's compensation division. (See listing in the back of the book for your state's information). The actual amount paid is based on the type of injury: temporary or permanent, total or partial disability.

For example, a worker may have sustained a permanent impairment, but may only qualify for partial disability. In such cases, the worker may only be able to return to his or her employment in a capacity that pays less. In such instances, worker's compensation is supposed to pay the difference between what was earned prior to the injury and what is earned after the job-related accident or injury, according to Wisconsin Department of Workforce Development (DWD).

In addition to the weekly payout, workers may receive benefits in a lump sum settlement, based on the degree of impairment suffered, such as the loss of a limb due to a work-related accident. In cases where permanent and total incapacity is the end result, the lump sum settlement will take into account the worker's earnings and projected life expectancy.

There is no guarantee that workers will receive a lump sum. That determination is solely dependent on the insurance company and the judge as to whether the worker receives the money that way. When a lump sum is over $30,000, the judge could decide that a lump sum payout may not be in the best interest of the injured worker. This means the judge determines how much and when the worker can withdraw funds. Once the lump sum is disbursed, the remaining money is automatically deposited by the state to the bank of your choice. This is usually a personal savings account. The deposit is made on the same date every month determined by your state and the judge specified. The judge does this to protect the worker from spending all the money at one time, since this money is supposed to replace the worker's salary.

In our case, it was determined by Dennis's surgeon that he was 75 to 80 percent disabled according to the worker's compensation insurance company. In Wisconsin, this determination is made using a formula set by the DWD and utilized by the medical practitioner to calculate the extent of the disability.

Dennis was found to be 100-percent disabled by Social Security Disability. The federal government pays Social Security Disability to Americans who are unable to work. This is separate from worker's compensation and can be paid at the same time. Applying for Social Security Disability is a separate process from the worker's compensation and has separate rules and qualifications.

SOCIAL SECURITY DISABILITY

When you know you are permanently disabled, you can file for Social Security Disability. This is one of the largest federal programs assisting individuals who are disabled.

You and your doctor must first fill out an application. The agency will contact your doctor for information. The application is lengthy, so get prepared by gathering all your medical records, because you will be asked for details about doctor visits, dates of injury, as well as diagnosis. When completing the application, do not "brag" about what you are able to do, but rather, be completely honest about what you are unable to do.

People are often denied disability insurance the first time they submit their application. Often, people will hire an SSD attorney who is well versed in the process for assistance.

Social Security Disability is paid from a federal program and can be revoked if and when you recover from your disability. For more information about this program, visit www.ssa.gov/disability/.

Once Dennis was given his percentage of disability by his surgeon, our attorney was able to present these numbers to the judge and request a lump sum. Dennis had to present a plan for the money, and then the judge determined what we were allowed to have dispersed to us.

WHAT TO DO WHEN MEDICAL BILLS ARE NOT BEING PAID BY WORKER'S COMPENSATION

What is an injured worker to do when he or she has medical bills that are not being paid by the employer or the worker's compensation insurance carrier? What are injured workers supposed to do when they cannot return to work, pay their bills, or put food on the table for their families? Many of the blue-collar workers in this country have little legal knowledge. They are good people who are not looking to take advantage of their employers! They only want to work and support their families.

Are the attorneys getting paid for their services? Yes. Legitimate attorneys who specialize in worker's compensation cases take a restricted payment from the injured employee's settlement. In most states, this payment is 20 percent. Rarely do the attorneys require payment up front.

Review the worker's compensation information in your state and see if you want to take on this million-dollar industry by yourself.

Dennis and I chose not to, but every situation is different, as is every family and patient.

SO, WHO IS GETTING RICH FROM THE WORKER'S COMPENSATION SYSTEM?

Our nation's worker's compensation insurance system covers 127 million workers. It is regulated state by state with no federal oversight or assistance from Congress.

According to Robert P. Hartwig, chief economist at the Insurance Information Institute, the average cost of worker's compensation insurance paid by employers rose 50 percent between 2004-2007, and continues to rise. (Hartwig, 2012).

California has been a leader in worker's compensation reform and abuse. It has suffered one of the largest increases in premiums, which has led to lost jobs, decreased wages, and business closings.

Industry officials and governmental agencies claim that worker's compensation insurance rates are escalating because of rising medical and legal costs price, wars by insurers, insurance companies simple fighting for business and raising costs to their customers and according to insurers and businesses, fraud is also a contributing factor.

If you have researched any type of insurance rates over the past few years, premiums have all risen significantly. Worker's compensation insurance is a particular problem because its purchase is mandatory. While businesses seek to reduce expenses, they are limited because every employee must be fully insured with worker's compensation insurance. Nevertheless, some companies still choose not to carry this insurance because of the high premiums.

Worker's compensation insurance premiums are dependent on the type of business: the higher risk of injury on a job, the higher the premium. For companies in the construction industries, worker's compensation premiums are higher than a company that employs office staff.

Those who choose not to purchase worker's compensation insurance take their chances and hope employees will not get hurt or manipulate employees when injuries do occur. A filed claim can be devastating to both the employer and employee. When an employee gets injured on the job, but the employer does not have worker's compensation insurance, medical care can be delayed. A worker's income is often delayed, forcing the injured employee to file a personal claim against the employer, ultimately costing the employer more money for a larger claim and higher premiums.

During the mid-1990s, expenses for insurance companies dipped and profits skyrocketed, just like the securities and real estate markets. Today, after dropping their prices below the cost of covering claims in a fierce battle for market share, worker's compensation insurance companies are confronted with dismal returns on investment, which has resulted in astounding price increases as they pass these losses on to their customers. The premiums increased extremely after the insurance industry lost at least $40 billion in the terrorist attacks on Sept. 11 2001.

The insurance industry is not the only business trying to make money off injured workers. The healthcare industry is attempting to get its share of the revenue as well. Our country is shifting away from manufacturing jobs to less-dangerous service work. This, along with improvements in safety, has resulted in a drop in worker's compensation claims by 36 percent in the last decade, according to Occupational Injury Report. (*Occupational Injury Report,* online) However, the average medical cost per claim has nearly doubled.

Since the attacks of September 11, 2001, it has not been unusual to see business insurance premiums increase by as much as 70 percent in a single year. According to Joe Heidelmaier, vice president of City Sea Foods, in an article in the *New York Times,* his premiums jumped 68 percent in one year to $398,288, or an average of nearly $7,000 per worker. As a result, he planned to lay off approximately seven of his 57 employees.

Such increases are the cold, hard truth of what is happening in our country because of medical claims. Injured workers and businesses do not have any control or power over the amounts of insurance premiums. Please note that insurance companies or medical industries are not cutting employees—they are expanding. It is not just lost revenue that forces layoffs, but rather increased expenses that cannot be covered by revenues. Companies go into debt because of insurance premiums. Look at the size and elegance of the buildings being erected in your state by these two conglomerates. That should tell you exactly what their profits are like.

I believe that insurance companies and the medical industry are getting rich off of worker's compensation claims. While the insurance companies may allude to the fact that injured employees may be getting rich through fraud, in doing the research for this book, I did not see any wealthy employees. I found hard-working Americans losing their homes to foreclosure or having to claim bankruptcy because of medical bills that are not being paid by their insurance companies. Worst of all, I found people losing families through divorce because of the financial strain and emotional distress. Finally, when injured workers win their claims, the few years of wages are not worth it if one is 80 or 100 percent disabled.

THE WORKER'S COMPENSATION PROCESS

1. Incident report must be filed with Risk Services within 5 days of notification of injury from employee

2. Risk Services notifies Claims Administration

3. Claims administrator has 14 days (from the date of employer notification) to **Accept**, **Deny**, or **Delay** the claim. It is important for the supervisor is complete and submit the Incident Report Form within 24 hours of employee notification of an incident or injury.

    —Claim **denied**: No worker's compensation benefits provided.
    —Claim **delayed**: Claims administrator will contact employee and
        supervisor administrator has 90 days to determine
        compensabiity of the claim
        —Medical treatment with authorized is paid during delay
        —Wage loss / disability payments ... until claim is accepted
        —Independent medical evaluation (QME) may be performed to
            determine compensability

    —Claim **accepted**: Full extent of worker's compensation benefits as
            determined by statute:
        —Medical treatment
        —Transitional Return to Work
        —Temporary Work Assignment (TWA), which contains tasks
            consistent with employee work restrictions as
            provided to employee for up to 90 days in duration
            (May be shorter or longer depending on individual
            employee circumstances.)
        — Return to Regular work
            Employee continues ongoing medical treatment and is
            able to perform all essential functions of regular job
        —Total Temporary Disability (TTD)
            Employee is determined to be unable to perform his/
            her job duties by treating physician

4. Claim Resolution:

    —Employee discharged as cured
    —Permanent and stationary determination (P&S)
    —Decided by the treating physician or Qualified Medical Evaluator (QME)

    —If employee is determined to be P&S with work restrictions,
            there is an interactive process conducted to determine
            if employee can be accommodated
    —If permanent moderate or alternate work is offered within 30 days,
            then reduced PD payment.
    —If no modified or alternate work is offered within 30 days, then
            permanent disability (PD) rate increases and voucher may apply

*Please refer to your individual state regulations and worker's
compensation agency, as these are subject to change.*

Researchers say that the worker's compensation system has become such a dense patchwork of rules and regulations that seriously injured workers often need lawyers to guide them. Without the attorneys to interpret the maze, the workers may find themselves lost, alone, broke, and without a job.

The American worker's compensation system is very intimidating for an injured employee. As a healthcare worker, I initially attempted to find and interpret the rules and help my husband without looking for an attorney. However, the system is full of convoluted rules and regulations; and unless you know them in detail, it is the employee who runs the risk of losing everything to which he or she is entitled.

5. WORKING WITH WORKER'S COMPENSATION

ennis's employer committed worker's compensation insurance fraud when he refused to provide accurate information about the injury to the insurance provider. Don lied about how the injury had occurred, telling the worker's compensation insurance agent that Dennis never reported the injury and that he had injured himself at home while remodeling our home roofing and siding. I'm still amazed how anyone could do such a thing when Don actually saw his friend get injured and then pour that friend into his truck.

Don's misinformation resulted in the worker's compensation insurance company denying Dennis's original claim altogether. We were so naive. We believed that when a person was injured on the job, worker's compensation would pay for medical expenses incurred because of the injury. After all, that is what it is there for, right?

We were about to get a first-hand crash course in what worker's compensation really pays and does not pay and what laws it can circumvent. If the worker's compensation insurance company can avoid paying for anything, it will. It will also work very hard to deny any payments it can, for as long as it can, in the hope that the injured person will eventually give up trying to have legitimate medical bills paid.

I was mad! I was mad as hell! There was no way I would let my husband give up and allow the worker's compensation insurance company to win! I did not care what it took! At that time, in the early days of our battle, three weeks after Dennis's work-related injury, I had no idea how difficult the battle was going to be.

Our attorney told us that once we hired him, Dennis would be treated very differently. He was right. Suddenly Dennis no longer had a job. Technically, he hadn't been fired or let go from his job, but his employer refused to take him back to work. The excuse: the company was unable to accommodate work within his restrictions. The technical term used was "laid off," which meant Dennis lost all of his benefits, medical insurance, retirement benefits, vacation, holiday pay, and of course, wages.

Fortunately, Dennis was able to apply for unemployment benefits because he had been given permission to return to work with restrictions and his employer claimed there was no available work within his restrictions. Unemployment compensation was granted. Luckily, his employer did not fight the claim.

Our attorney was not thrilled about Dennis's receiving unemployment compensation, because it meant that when we did settle, unemployment would have to be paid back from the worker's compensation settlement. For us, a settlement felt like it was a million years away and our bills needed to be paid now. We took the unemployment compensation and decided to deal with the repayment on the back end.

We were looking at a court date that was over a year away. Normally, if worker's compensation denies a claim, it takes twelve or more months before a trial date is set. This timeline varies by state and the number of cases ahead of yours.

Fast forward to about eight months after Dennis got injured. We were facing major medical bills and his employer refused to provide health insurance. Despite our repeated efforts, the worker's compensation insurance company also refused to pay for any of the medical bills, lost wages, or pain medication. Such payments would have at least allowed us some financial breathing room, so Dennis could heal after surgery without worrying about the finances.

Because we had been unsuccessful in getting the worker's compensation insurance company to acknowledge and thus pay for medical treatment, we only had one option for covering the costs of the $100,000 back surgery. Dennis would have to apply for COBRA insurance.

Under federal law, when an employee is laid off, employers must offer COBRA, or Consolidated Omnibus Budget Reconciliation Act of 1985. This law requires most employers with group health insurance plans to offer employees the opportunity to continue their group health-care coverage temporarily under their employer's plan if their coverage otherwise would cease due to termination, layoff, or other change in employment status. This insurance could continue for up to eighteen months after employment. Employees are required to pay the premium on the insurance, but can keep the health coverage until they find another job that offers them insurance or they are able to obtain insurance coverage through a spouse.

Because Dennis's employer terminated his position, our entire family was no longer covered by its corporate medical plan. This left us in a place where we needed to find a new insurance carrier that would not see Dennis's injury as a preexisting condition. If it were considered preexisting, it would be excluded from coverage.

COBRA insurance is not cheap and it cost us $500 a month to cover just Dennis. If we had chosen to cover our entire family, the monthly cost would have been around $1,800. Luckily, I was able to obtain a separate policy for our children and myself at a reasonable cost. Could I have placed Dennis on my insurance and paid the higher deductible? Sure, but that would have significantly increased the premiums for my business. Why should my company pay for something that Dennis's employer should be covering? At least, that is how I saw things at the beginning of our journey.

Can you believe it? A doctor without medical insurance, in America? Many people think that doctors and nurses have the best healthcare benefits because they are in the business. Well, nothing could be farther from the truth. A doctor in private practice is like any other small business. It is difficult to get reasonable medical insurance rates because of the low numbers of employees. The companies are too small to negotiate good rates and benefit amounts.

SURVIVING THE FINANCIAL DOWNFALL

It was during the ninth month after Dennis's injury when I was really beginning to wonder how on earth we were going to handle all the medical and financial challenges. These challenges kept coming at every turn and twist. Somehow, however, we were able to find a way to make the best out of a bad situation.

One of the major challenges when a person becomes injured is the financial strain that comes along with the physical problems. It is no secret that our economy is in trouble. Americans are living paycheck to paycheck with more debt than ever before, and many of us are all only one disaster away from bankruptcy.

When situations like ours hit you in the face, the economic situation becomes more than just a news story you hear on the radio or TV. You empathize with anyone who is in such dire straits. Perhaps part of you believes that people should know better than to get into that much debt. I know, because I have felt that way too from time to time. The American lifestyle has become one in which we often live beyond our means. We want everything now; waiting is not in our mindset.

Looking back, I think we were very blessed. We had everything: a house with a hobby farm, a cottage in Northern Wisconsin, two vehicles, boats, and ATVs. We also had money in the bank, both of us had retirement savings, and we were not living paycheck to paycheck. Of course, we had debt as well. We had credit card bills and owed on the properties and cars. Please do not think for one minute that we had a life without financial issues. It seemed that we had really just gotten ourselves financially set—it had taken us sixteen years of marriage and a lot of hard work to get there.

When Dennis was injured and laid off, we lost his $50,000-a-year salary. We were worried about how we were going to hold our lifestyle together financially. We still had bills to pay and food to put on the table, and although there was money in the bank, it was far from a gold mine. Now we had less income coming in and more money going out than before Dennis's injury. No matter how we did the math, there is still less. We had one child entering college and two younger children who still needed clothes and school supplies. We had daily expenses that needed to be covered.

WHAT TO DO IF THIS HAPPENS TO YOU

First and foremost, if I can give you a piece of advice, make sure you have short-term and long-term disability insurance coverage. This will protect you so that if you do get injured, you have income that will help you pay your bills. You *cannot* apply for this insurance coverage after an injury. If we had had disability insurance, it would have helped us pay our bills and reduced our financial stress.

If you find yourself in a similar financial position, call your creditors early on and explain what has happened. Ask them to work with you. See if you can get assistance from family or friends. As hard as it might be, you might have to liquidate some of your assets to keep important things, like your house. Remember—it is only stuff and can always be replaced.

Dennis was very worried about how we would survive financially. He knew that my salary was not going to be enough to cover all our expenses. He just could not wait to be cleared to go back to work.

WORKER'S COMPENSATION SURVEILLANCE

Injured workers struggle financially and medically, but when worker's compensation insurance is involved, they also have to deal with private investigators following them, sitting outside their homes with cameras and video recorders, and worse—trying to verify that the injured persons are not actually injured so the insurance company does not have to pay the claim.

Of course, there are people out there trying to defraud the worker's compensation company, but they are far and few between. If the worker's compensation insurance company discovers that someone is pretending, the entire worker's compensation claim can be thrown out or denied. If a person files a fraudulent worker's compensation claim, he or she could be prosecuted for fraud, would then face legal charges, and have to pay back any money back received.

I remember one night, Dennis and I were taking a walk and a little blue pick-up truck with a camera attached to the window went by. We knew that the "spy" was from the worker's compensation insurance company. We were certainly not doing anything wrong, but it still made us nervous. I think it's just human nature to become anxious when being watched.

The next day, I called our attorney to inform him about what happened. He was not in the least surprised and informed us that the little blue truck was just the beginning and we could expect more of such surveillance in the future. I was shocked! Our attorney proceeded to educate me about the rules and that legally; private investigators hired by the workers compensation insurance company had the right to follow us as long as they complied with the rules.

The US Patriot Act gave law enforcement officials sweeping new powers to conduct searches without warrants, monitor financial transactions, and eavesdrop. They can detain and deport, in secret, individuals suspected of committing terrorist acts. (Congress, 2001)

Also be aware that the worker's compensation insurance company is smart and has more money and resources than private individuals. It is therefore not unusual for the worker's compensation insurance company to hire more than one person. In addition, the private investigator (PI) will likely use more than one vehicle. It is also common for the worker's compensation insurance company to hire multiple investigators so that injured parties under surveillance will not get used to seeing the same person or vehicle.

If the investigator feels the tree line is public property, he or she can sneak up in there and get close enough to take pictures, at a better angle, of the happenings inside your house. Yes, this is legal!

Find out about the surveillance rules in your state, and make sure worker's comp-hired investigators are not invading your privacy or causing you any danger. If they are in violation of your personal rights, call the authorities and call your attorney.

Remember to document everything! I kept a special notebook to record when and where the investigators sat, what types of car they drove, along with a description of each PI.

Being followed by the little blue surveillance truck was only the first of many such experiences. Over the next year, we knew of at least five different people and vehicles watching our home. They would park across the street from our house. We live in the country and trees surround our home. In summer, you cannot see our home from the road. The only way someone would be able to get a photo is if he or she were stationed directly across from our driveway, which would be impossible because we live on a rural, one-lane street. I often asked myself what they thought they would see through the trees, but they must have thought there was something. For all I know, they had special equipment that allowed them photographic access.

Several investigators actually climbed up our private hillside from the road and took pictures of our son working with his steer. They must have thought it was Dennis. It completely frightened our 11-year-old son. The first time it happened, he came running into the house, saying someone was in the bushes. After we explained what was going on, he began throwing cow manure over the hill, so if investigators decided to climb up, they would have a surprise. Not a bad idea. I wish I had thought of it.

HERE'S WHAT YOU NEED TO KNOW ABOUT WORKER'S COMPENSATION COMPANY "SPIES"

The rules are apparently made to be broken for worker's comp-hired private investigators. They cannot come onto your private property, but they can park directly in front of your home or driveway.

They are allowed to follow you in their vehicle, but cannot drive erratically.

They can take pictures of you in any form or in any place they chose. They can use any type of photographic equipment manufactured. This means they can sit outside and view directly inside your home. Keep your window shades drawn if you do not want them to see you naked or having sex, or even just relaxing at home.

Nothing is private once you file a worker's comp claim. President George W. Bush changed this privacy act after 9/11. Thanks a lot.

Our children are quite bold so they would approach the investigators and ask if they were lost or needed help. The PIs would leave soon after being approached. Dennis also told our local police that someone was watching our home; he was concerned that they were taking pictures of our family, and specifically our daughter. While this might not have been quite kosher, we were learning to fight fire with fire and not take the surveillance lying down. We all teach our children to be aware of strangers and not to talk to them or approach them. It is your right to protect your family.

6. THINGS TO KNOW, STEPS TO TAKE WHEN YOU'RE INJURED

M any questions arise when one is injured at work. Below are a few of the basic questions commonly asked when a worker is injured on the job, based on advice provided by two organizations that help injured workers: www.workerscompensation.com and www.disabilitysecrets.com.

WHO PAYS THE MEDICAL BILLS?

If your claim is found to be work-related and the employer's worker's compensation insurance carrier agrees, then your medical bills will be paid by the worker's compensation insurance company.

Keep careful track of any medical bills and when and how they are paid. If you pay any bills yourself, keep copies of all payments so that you can submit for reimbursement from the worker's compensation insurance company later.

When you receive medical care, you must tell the doctor's office your worker's compensation case number, insurance carrier, address, and phone number, along with the name of your case worker if you want your claims to be paid. Also, provide the office with your private medical insurance information in case worker's compensation decides not to pay for services.

The worker's compensation insurance company can dispute any medical claims if it feels your injuries are not work-related. To prevent this from happening, only discuss your work-related injury during any doctor's visits being paid by worker's compensation insurance.

WHAT IF MY CLAIM IS DISPUTED?

A disputed claim could occur between you, the employer, and/or the insurer. For example, your employer feels your injury did not occur on the job or the insurance company may determine that your injury is different than the diagnosis you received from your healthcare provider. If the disputed claim cannot be settled, you may request a hearing to resolve it before an administrative law judge who may issue an order.

If your employer does not report your accident, or if you believe you can prove that you did not receive all your benefits, you may file an application for a hearing to challenge the disputed claim. There must be medical proof of your claim. This proof is in the form of a written opinion of a physician, chiropractor, psychologist, physician assistant, advanced practice nurse prescriber, podiatrist, or surgeon. The medical report must accompany the application.

It is important to talk with your employer and the insurer before applying for a hearing to understand exactly what portion of the claim is being disputed.

WHAT IF I AM UNABLE TO RETURN TO MY JOB?

Unfortunately, some workers are unable to return to the same type of work they performed before the injury or illness. It is important to stay in contact with your employer and your medical practitioner to determine when you can return to work and if your employer will consider taking you back with restrictions, possibly in a modified job if necessary. This can potentially ease you back into work.

If your practitioner or employer indicates that you cannot return to your former job, you may contact the insurer to request assistance from either public or private vocational rehabilitation services.

In Wisconsin, the State Division of Vocational Rehabilitation (DVR) has offices throughout the state and can be contacted through the State Department of Workforce Development. There is a listing of all state offices at the back of this book. General questions about your claim should be addressed to your employer, its insurer, or your state's Worker's Compensation Division.

If you reach your healing plateau and are unable to obtain a job, you can apply for unemployment insurance benefits. If you decide to proceed and file for a hearing, contact the Worker's Compensation Division offices for specific details in your state. You will also receive additional written information explaining the hearing process. If you cannot return to your current position, I would recommend you contact an attorney who specializes in Worker's compensation injuries.

WHAT IF MY EMPLOYER CHOOSES NOT TO REHIRE ME?

In Wisconsin, the law, according to the state Workforce Development, does not guarantee you a job after you become an injured worker, and your employer is not required to hold a position open or create one. Your employer is required to provide suitable work and return you to the job you left, or offer an equivalent job, provided that such a position is available.

However, going back to work in a light-duty capacity may mean that you still need to be paid worker's compensation benefits to make up the difference for what you would have earned in your regular position. Be aware that some employers will claim they do not have light-duty employment available simply so they can stop paying worker's compensation benefits.

Therefore, avoid being overzealous in your desire to return to work. Moreover, you should not attempt to play down your symptoms when speaking with any healthcare providers who are managing your recovery. The unfortunate truth is that even though you sincerely wish to return to work, you may discover that your employer does not have your best interests at heart.

Workers may be entitled to a maximum of one year's back pay if an employer "unreasonably refuses" to rehire the injured worker. Workers who believe they have been unreasonably refused employment should request a hearing and contact an attorney.

WHAT HAPPENS IF I LOSE A WORKER'S COMPENSATION CASE AT ARBITRATION?

Typically, an appeal can be filed and the employer can continue to provide your worker's compensation benefits. However, the longer a case drags on, the worse it can be for you, since you are only receiving worker's compensation, two-thirds of your normal wages. It is therefore not unusual for injured workers to deplete their personal savings after a worker's compensation claim has been filed.

When Dennis was injured and worker's compensation did not pay for his medical expenses or cover his lost wages, initially we used our personal savings to cover our expenses and our private health insurance took care of his medical expenses. Our attorney filed an appeal on our behalf when the worker's compensation insurance denied coverage for Dennis's claim.

One thing we have learned about arbitration and hearings is that the worker's compensation insurance companies will bring in anything they possibly can to win a case, even if it is not one hundred percent accurate.

WHAT IF I AM PERMANENTLY DISABLED?

If you are permanently disabled from an injury sustained at work, the worker's compensation insurance company will have to pay you. If you think you will be paid a great deal of money for the rest of your life, think again. The worker's compensation insurance industry has an injury scale to assess a percentage of disability. Payment for permanent or partial disability is based on 1000 weeks of pay.

For example, a worker has a work-related lumbar-disc injury that is considered a 10-percent injury on the worker's compensation injury scale. The scale is based on 1000 weeks, so 10 percent of permanent total disability (PTD) equals 100 weeks of pay from the insurance company.

WHAT IF I AM TOTALLY DISABLED?

If you are found totally disabled, you will be able to collect from worker's compensation insurance, along with Social Security Disability

What is Disability?

- **Temporary disability**, in which it is likely that the injured worker will be able to resume gainful employment with no or only partial disability. The ability to return to work relates only to work with the company that employed the worker at the time of the accident.

A temporary disability can be classified as either a *temporary total disability* or *temporary partial disability*.

A *temporary total disability* means the worker is not able to work at all for a period of time, but is expected to recover fully.

A *temporary partial disability* means the worker is capable of light or part-time duties.

- The amount of compensation is typically a percentage of an employee's wages during a maximum period of time.

(Source: Occupational Safety and Health, David L. Goetsch)

Insurance (SSDI), as discussed in the previous chapter. There are limits on the amount of money you can collect from both, so if possible, wait to apply for SSDI until your worker's compensation claim is settled. The pay scale is also determined in terms of weeks, as is true of any other disabilities. The worker's compensation insurance company will fight you for sure! Its goal is to try and get you to settle the claim for the least amount of money.

HOW LONG IS MY CLAIM OPEN?

Your claim remains open until you and the worker's compensation insurance company come to a decision on the settlement. This can take a few months or a few years. If (when) you end up in court and win your case, your case could be appealed for years before a settlement is actually reached. Most people will negotiate a claim that still keeps their medical claim open. This means that the medical part of the claim can stay open for 12 years, according to the Wisconsin Department of Workforce Development, and means that future medical treatments will be covered if they are needed. However, it does not mean that the worker's compensation insurance company will not deny needed medical treatment if it deems treatment is not related to the work injury.

7. WHAT HAPPENS ONCE YOU HIRE AN ATTORNEY

I t is important to understand that once an injured worker decides to hire an attorney, the relationship between the worker and the employer will never be the same. This decision must be carefully considered. I am certainly not trying to discourage anyone from hiring an attorney, because in many cases, I believe that the worker's interests can be protected with a worker's compensation attorney. However, I have also heard of many problems that have occurred with injured workers who hired attorneys. I have researched the literature and want to provide you with some information to help you determine if hiring an attorney is right for you.

Here are two examples. A California resident was injured on the job. His Human Resource department sent him a letter stating he would always have a job with the company—until he hired an attorney to represent him for his worker's compensation injury. He then received a letter from the HR department stating he no longer had a job. Another gentleman who fell at work, injuring his ankle, was let go three weeks later because he could not do the job he was hired for anymore while he was recovering from his work-related injury.

If your work injuries are relatively minor and the expectation is that the impairments will not leave permanent damage, there may be little need to hire a worker's compensation attorney. However, if the work-related injury is serious and the worker's compensation insurance carrier rejects your claim, hiring an attorney who specializes in worker's compensation claims may be the best course of action. Also, an attorney may be helpful in the following instances:

- Your claim is accepted. However, the correct payment is not received.

- Your employer retaliates against you after the worker's compensation claim is filed with disciplinary action or outright firing. Be prepared for the retaliation from your employer, who may not appreciate you filling a case against the company. It will cost your employer money and time. In addition, your employer might need to hire someone to replace you while still paying you.

- The worker's compensation insurance carrier denies medical care for your injury.

Worker's compensation cases may be adversarial and since consultations with worker's compensation lawyers are often free, it is probably in your best interest to discuss your case with a qualified attorney before doing anything independently.

Having a worker's compensation attorney handle your case can often ensure that you are treated fairly and given appropriate financial consideration with regard to your injury or illness. Unfortunately, it has been my experience that an attorney cannot expedite the case with regard to payments. However, an attorney can be of great assistance in maneuvering your case and getting a date for a hearing more quickly.

Choose an attorney who specializes in worker's compensation claims and can provide you with a history of cases and outcomes. Do not be afraid to ask for the attorney's history. You are hiring the attorney and he or she should not hesitate to tell you what results have been achieved.

I would also recommend that you check out the attorney you want to hire through your state's Department of Licensing. This licensing department will tell you if the attorney is currently licensed, though it is unlikely that you will be able to find a chart or graph of an attorney's wins and losses record. It is possible to put something together through public records searches, or through legal research services like Westlaw and LexisNexis.

HOW TO FIND THE RIGHT
WORKER'S COMPENSATION ATTORNEY

You can find worker's compensation attorneys through advertisements, your state's bar association, online, or even the Yellow Pages. If you know someone who has also had a worker's compensation claim, inquire as to whether or not the person was represented by an attorney. Seek a referral from someone you know who worked with an attorney and was pleased.

If you cannot obtain a qualified referral for a potential attorney, interview more than one attorney to determine who is best qualified to handle your claim. Good communication and good rapport between you and the attorney are key in this relationship.

When you meet with an attorney for the first time, make sure you are prepared for the meeting. Write down your questions in advance, and then during the meeting, take notes and write down the attorney's answers as well. This way, you can refer to your notes instead of having to call him/her back. A few good questions are:

- "How long have you been practicing worker's compensation law?"

- "What is your fee?" Remember, it should be 20 percent because that is law for worker's compensation cases.

- "Do you require any money up front to work the case?"
  Attorneys who are good at what they do should not require money up front for a worker's compensation case. When an attorney is paid up front, the motivating factor—money—is gone. If the attorney gets paid when you get paid, he or she is more likely to work faster and harder for you.

- It is appropriate to ask for references. "What is your track record for settling these types of cases?"

Once you decide on an attorney, you can expect to have an initial, face-to-face meeting to completely discuss your case and determine if there is legal precedence to proceed with your case. Once you officially hire your attorney, most of your contact will be via phone or letters to explain what is occurring with the case until your court date. Keep the attorney updated on any specific medical information or changes in your condition so that he or she stays current with your situation.

Before any decisions are made about applying for Social Security Disability Insurance, unemployment compensation, or returning to work, discuss these with your attorney. It is important that you completely understand how applying for these services can affect your worker's compensation claim. It may not seem important at the time, but trust me, in the end, the decisions could mean a great deal of money to you.

Also, be aware that whatever you do during the time you are waiting to settle will come up during your trial. For example, if you do not follow through with doctors' recommendations for treatment, or if you return to work before your work restrictions are lifted, these will be used against you.

Your attorney will ask you to keep records of all bills and expenses related to your injury that have not been paid by the worker's compensation insurance company. Start a notebook or computer record to write down details about the situation. Start keeping notes as soon as the injury occurs, because it is amazing how easy it is to forget the details as time passes. If you haven't begun your record keeping until today, start now and write down as much as you can remember, dates, meetings, and so on.

I started by keeping a document on my laptop that included the date of the injury, witnesses, any medical appointments, doctors' names, as well as phone calls and conversations between the employer and us. These records came in very handy, especially since our case took almost three years to settle; it is impossible to remember all the fine details.

A word of advice—if you are going to keep your records on a computer—make sure you back up the files. You could be keeping records for several years and while no one expects the computer to crash, it might happen and the documentation for your case could be lost.

It is up to you to work with your attorney as much as possible. You should provide your attorney with the most accurate information. If your attorney sends you paperwork, complete it and return it within an appropriate timeframe. Sign the release of records that your attorney needs to obtain information on your healthcare.

When things change with your case, inform your attorney immediately. To help you as much as possible, your attorney needs to know the specific details about any changes. You are a team and together you can beat the system. Together you will protect yourself and others from future injuries and mistreatment.

8. DENNIS'S FIRST SURGICAL PROCEDURE

D ennis and I were so hopeful as we prepared for the first surgical procedure. The surgeon—let's call him Dr. Jones—told us he was going to use synthetic recombinant bone inside cages and screws on Dennis's back. I began to research the surgical procedure the doctor was going to perform. A website, www.spinal-health.com, was recommended by the surgeon to provide us with all the information we needed to know about the surgery.

Dr. Jones also gave us the names of two patients Dennis could talk with before his surgery. One patient had a positive outcome and one patient had a negative outcome. The patients who Dennis was calling had provided a written consent to release their information. Dennis proceeded to call these patients to discuss the surgery and their recovery experiences. He felt that he had enough information to make his decision regarding surgery. I felt it was important for Dennis to talk directly to the people who had undergone this type of surgery, and I provided my husband with some basic questions to ask each of the men. However, I did not talk to either patient directly.

When you talk with people who have undergone similar operations as the one being proposed, a few questions to ask are:

- "What type of procedure did you have?"
  If you are getting information from someone who did not have the same procedure, you are not comparing apples to apples.

- "How did you feel after the surgery? "

- "How long did it take you to recover?"

- "Did you smoke after your surgery?"

- "Would you do the surgery again?"

- "Do you feel the surgery helped with your symptoms?"

The plan was for Dennis to undergo an anterior lumbar interbody fusion (ALIF). This procedure entails entering the spine from the abdomen to place cages and screws in the appropriate spaces. The surgery would take several hours and require a two- or three-day stay at the hospital.

Normally, while discussing surgical consent, a physician will provide information about the benefits and risks involved with the surgical procedure to the patient. He or she will also provide written information for the patient to review. In our case, the only consent information provided to us was that this particular procedure would be done with synthetic recombinant bone and it was the best option at this time. We were told this procedure and product were 90 percent effective. We were also told this surgery would prevent Dennis from having to undergo a second surgery.

The other typical option with an injury such as Dennis's would be to harvest bone from the patient's hip and transplant this into the spine as a graft for the fusion. Our surgeon informed us that the recombinant bone was better than undergoing another surgery. We were never given options, but instead, were told what would be done.

We were only given the option of the synthetic graft and told it was the best option. We never signed a consent form for surgery in the clinic.

I searched the Internet and Dennis and I reviewed any videos available so we could see exactly what would happen. The information I found about synthetic recombinant bone led me to a product called Infuse® and cardiac grafts. In 2007, I was not able to find any negative information regarding this product; it had been FDA-approved for use in patients with surgical procedures. As I am writing this book, Infuse® is undergoing legal battles for causing bone deterioration and increased risk of cancer.

Being the researcher I am, we returned to Dr. Jones's office with questions in hand regarding the procedure itself, the recovery time, and any potential side effects that he could foresee. At that time, Dr. Jones's only concern was that Dennis was a smoker; the surgeon told us he would not to do the surgical procedure if Dennis was still smoking the day of surgery. Smoking can reduce the blood flow and disrupt the healing process, ultimately preventing a fusion from occurring. Dennis agreed to quit smoking to undergo the surgical procedure, but in fact, was not able to quit prior to his surgery and even continued to be smoke for several months after the operation.

In retrospect, trusting our surgeon was the first mistake we made. We were so happy to have a surgeon who believed what we were telling him that we never thought of getting a second opinion about the procedure. After all, in the six months that had passed since Dennis's injury, we had already gotten five different opinions about the injury; no one has

A fusion is a surgical technique in which one or more of the vertebrae of the spine are united together ("fused") so that motion no longer occurs between them. This frontal X-ray of the lumbar spine shows post-operative changes with pedicle screw fixation at L4 and L5 and an interbody fusion cage between L4 and L5. (ScienceSource 2014).

been able to help relieve any of the pain or explain the reason for his pain.

Dennis and I both agreed to go ahead with the ALIF surgery. Dennis could not continue with the pain he was in for the rest of his life. He just wanted to get better. So we scheduled the surgery for March 9, 2007. We were planning a full recovery for turkey hunting season, which was a few weeks away and the excitement was already in the air for our family. With positive attitudes and a positive mindset, we prepared for surgery day.

When we entered the hospital, Dennis was taken to the surgical holding room. Dr. Jones's physician assistant came in to prepare us for what was about to occur. He asked if there were any final questions before surgery and gave us his positive thoughts that everything would be better when this was over. Dennis was handed a hospital consent form and asked to sign so they could move forward with the surgery, as they were running late.

Two nurses began to wheel Dennis into the operating room. Doing what he was told, he briefly glanced over the consent form, signed it, and handed the clipboard back to the nurse as they opened the doors to the operating room.

According to the California state bar, a study published in 2011 showed that medical errors occur in one-third of hospital admissions, as much as ten times more common than previously estimated.

Since 2000, the Food and Drug Administration (FDA) has received more than 95,000 reports of medication errors.

Several hours later, Dennis woke up in the recovery room with an abdominal incision, cages drilled into two discs in his spine and something called recombinant bone put into the cages to assist with fusion of the spine. We had been told this product was superior compared to human bone or Dennis's own bone. Later, we would find out that this statement was no more than a lie and the product used was no more effective than snake oil!

When we arrived at the hospital, I had told the nursing staff that I was planning on spending the night with him; they were wonderful at trying to make my stay as comfortable as possible. They provided me with a roll-away bed to sleep on and offered me food and drink.

If you have a loved one in the hospital, stay with the person as long as you can. When a loved one is ill, it is difficult for that person to advocate for himself or herself, or communicate exactly what is needed. Be your loved one's voice. Ensure that he or she gets what is needed for comfort—and do your best to protect your loved one from potential medical errors.

I am in the healthcare industry and we are all human; errors occur. You can be there to remind the medical staff of possible allergies or potential interactions and definitely report any unusual changes in your loved one's behavior or appearance. This could save your loved one from potentially deadly errors!

When Dennis opened his eyes for the first time after the surgery, he immediately knew something was wrong. He stared at me with a frightened look on his face and said it felt like someone had hit him in the back with a baseball bat.

Throughout that first night, I assisted in nursing my husband and tried to encourage him. It turned out that he had not received the right type of pain medication. Several times during the night, a male nurse came in to check on Dennis, and we repeatedly told the nurse that Dennis's pain was out control. The nurse checked Dennis's vitals and provided him with some ice, but that was it.

Finally, at 7 o'clock the next morning, a new shift nurse arrived. She listened to us and brought a different type of IV (intravenous) pain medication for Dennis. It was the first time in 24 hours that he was able to experience a reduction in his pain, but it still was not gone completely. After a few hours, he was put on oral pain medication in an attempt to control the horrible pain.

Our hospital experience only became more dramatic when we found out that the hospital was full and they were admitting pneumonia patients on the surgical floor! This infuriated me!

The cardinal rule for fresh surgical patients is keeping them away from infection; their immune systems are weakened and they are at high risk for infection. This is especially true with spinal patients; the last thing you want is an infection in the spine.

When Dr. Jones came in for the first time after surgery, Dennis requested that he be discharged from the hospital. I could take care of him at home, where his risk of infection would be significantly reduced. So at 11 o'clock that night, I drove him to our home, an hour away from the hospital.

There were many reasons for removing Dennis from the hospital as quickly as possible. People often heal better at home than they do in a hospital. I would not recommend this to every family, but if you have some medical training or assistance, this might be a good option for you. As a healthcare practitioner, I knew what I was looking for in the way of infection, I could change his dressings, and monitor for pain control. The biggest reason for us leaving the hospital was the pneumonia issue, which was completely uncalled for and irresponsible, as far as I was concerned.

Once we returned home, Dennis suffered terribly with sciatica, pain that radiated down his leg. We could not find a single position that made him comfortable. His pain level was still rated a 9 out of 10 three days after surgery with use of narcotic pain medication. When I called the surgeon's office, the receptionist connected me to the physician's assistant. I explained what was happening and he was nice enough to call our home to talk with Dennis. The PA immediately ordered an MRI.

Going for the MRI was yet another ordeal. We had to drive to a facility 90 minutes away, one way. Dennis could barely sit for ten minutes, let alone ride in a bumpy car in an uncomfortable position for the long ride.

The drive was just the beginning. Once we got to the MRI center, we had to wait forty minutes to be seen. Dennis was then expected to lie flat for the MRI procedure. Dennis could not lie flat, especially for twenty minutes. He did the best he could and the staff worked very hard to get the MRI reading done as quickly as possible.

Dennis certainly needed pain meds after that. Unfortunately, we had left them at home and we had another torturous 90-minute ride back.

In truth, we would not have had to drive that far. We had a hospital twenty minutes away; the only reason we had gone to the more distant facility was because our surgeon had a relationship with that facility. We could have requested to go to the closer hospital. This may sound like common sense, but when you are caring for your loved ones, you go into auto-mode and just do what you are told. If you are going to be a good advocate, ask lots of questions and analyze the answers you get before you agree to things.

> Keep your pain medication (and other important medication) with you at all times.

During the first post-operative visit, Dennis saw the physician's assistant, who told us the pain Dennis was experiencing was normal. The PA never looked at the incision, which was on Dennis's abdomen, but documented that he had a back incision that was healing well.

I would not have known this was documented inappropriately if I had not have requested a copy of the medical records. In fact, I did not request records until Dennis was *not* recovering. (Today, I question whether that was intentional or "simply" a medical error).

Dennis was given a prescription for a drug called Neurontin®, also known as Gabapentin®, an antiseizure medication used to treat nerve pain as well. He tried this for a short time, but unfortunately, it provided no relief and the mood shifts and behavior-related side effects were unbearable. Dennis became irritable, was drowsy most of the time, and became aggressive—completely different from my husband under normal circumstances. Dennis gradually weaned himself off this medication.

He suffered for several weeks and we were unable to control the nerve pain, which had begun to radiate down his right leg, causing him to walk with an extreme limp. Dennis and I truly tried everything to heal and recover properly. He was so tired of being in pain and not being himself—he just wanted this to all be over.

When it came time for the first follow-up visit with Dr. Jones, it was a pleasant meeting with minimal small talk and a little explanation about the surgery. We were told that everything on the MRI showed that Dennis's back was healing well. He was told to keep doing what he was doing. Dennis worried that maybe he was overdoing his activities and that was causing so much pain. I am not sure where that idea came from, because at that point, Dennis was only walking back and forth to the end of our 80-yard long driveway a few times a day.

Dr. Jones told Dennis to do whatever felt comfortable, because it was impossible to break anything. Everything had been fixed. There was a brief discussion about sciatica, and we were told such nerve pain was normal and could last several months.

Each subsequent doctor's visit was the same—small talk to rule out depression, and occasionally a quick look at his back and how he moved. The visits were always pleasant and the surgeon took ample time to answer our questions.

Three months after the surgery, Dennis was still complaining about pain and his inability to move without considerable discomfort. He was offered an additional surgery to place rods in this back to stabilize his back. Our surgeon told us the problem was that the fusion was not healing as well as it should. He could not guarantee a second surgery would relieve Dennis's pain either. We were quite confused, because prior to this date, we had been told that everything was healing well.

I remember leaving the doctor's office in a state of shock. During all prior visits, we had been told that Dennis was healing well and that the bones were fusing properly. Why would they want to perform another surgery?

Dennis made his decision in less than 24 hours. It was a firm NO! No more surgeries! He felt if the doctors could not fix him the first time, there would be no way they could fix him a second time. I could not argue with this thought process. I immediately called the doctor's office and explained Dennis's decision. They respected this choice and told us to follow up in one month as usual.

RECOMMENDATIONS FOR FINDING A HEALTHCARE PRACTITIONER AND FACILITY

You have been injured at work. Now it is time to seek medical care. If you have a primary care practitioner, you should call your doctor and schedule an appointment right away. When you call for the appointment, make sure you tell the scheduler that the appointment is for a worker's compensation injury. The scheduler or billing clerk will ask specific questions regarding the injury, such as date of the injury, your employer, and its worker's compensation insurance company, along with the case number.

When you arrive for the appointment, you will be asked questions about how the injury occurred, and what you felt before and after the injury. It is important that you are specific and honest. Do not overinflate the symptoms or the incident.

If you have to see other practitioners for your care, make sure you explain the details of your injury the same way with each healthcare practitioner. This is important because the worker's compensation insurance company will look for inconsistencies in your story between the different practitioners. Unfortunately, you do not have control over how these practitioners document what you tell them.

If your practitioner schedules testing or follow-up appointments, make sure you attend all of them or reschedule with a good reason.

FREQUENTLY ASKED QUESTIONS

What if I don't have a doctor?
If you do not have a healthcare practitioner, you may need to receive immediate care at an urgent care clinic or the emergency room. Ask family and friends for recommendations, and what they like or dislike about their physicians or other healthcare providers. It is important to find the best care you can; it should not matter if the practitioner is someone in your network or not—you are looking for the best one to deal with your particular injury.

What if I don't like the hospital / location?

You must also speak up and advocate for yourself; if you cannot, find someone who can. If you need hospital services, you must feel comfortable with the facility at which you will be receiving care. If you are uncomfortable with the hospital with which your practitioner is affiliated, make sure you discuss this with your doctor in detail.

In our case, we were sent an hour and half away from our home for an MRI and I did not speak up. Having to travel such a distance when it was so painful for Dennis to sit for that long didn't make sense, because our local hospital, which has MRI equipment, was only twenty minutes away. Advocate for a more convenient or suitable location early on. Do not make the mistakes I made.

What if I don't like the doctor?

Your choice of healthcare practitioners is extremely important in your recovery. If you feel that a particular practitioner is not helping you or the two of you are not communicating appropriately, then it is time to "fire" that person and find someone else to work with. Feeling comfortable with and trusting your practitioner(s) is necessary for your recovery! Do not hesitate—this is your life, your body, and your livelihood!

Can I ask for my medical records?

Ask for copies of all your medical records and notes after each visit. You have the right to see and have these. After every visit, review the records immediately and check for any inconsistencies. After a few months, it is easy to forget exactly how you felt. Making sure each doctor visit is properly documented can make or break your case.

In our situation, when I reviewed our medical records several years later, I found blatant inaccuracies, but it was too late to change Dennis's records. Such inaccuracies included: "patient is healing well with remarkable decrease in pain." I read this and knew that was not true, but it is too late to change it.

Nor did the records contain any mention that I was a healthcare practitioner. I did not think this was relevant until we were in court and the opposing lawyer used my profession against me, trying to say I was hiding things from our surgeon. I had told our surgeon about my profession, but it was not documented, so it became a "he said / she said" scenario. I actually began to question if I had told the surgeon I was a practitioner or not. I had told all our doctors that I was a practitioner, so why would I have hidden this information from Dr. Jones?

Should I get a second opinion?
Get multiple opinions about the injury and how best to treat it. If you can, get as many as three or four different medical opinions. This may be difficult because Worker's compensation insurance only allows you to have one doctor at a time and it may appear that you are "doctor shopping." Remember, this is your life or the life of a loved one. You have a right to protect yourself and feel comfortable with what is recommended to you!

Do I have to take notes?
Keep records of all your doctor visits. Doctors make notes in your medical records and you can do the same thing. Write down the dates and names of people you speak with, especially insurance company conversations! You also want to document all your conversations with your employer. Keeping good records will save you problems if and when you have to go to court to fight your case for worker's compensation.

Date	Doctors Name & Location	Conversation
1/10/06	Dr. Feel Good, Milwaukee, WI	Dr. Feel Good would like me to have an MRI. I asked why this would be done and what is he hoping to find. After the MRI when would I be able to get the results?

More importantly, ***DO NOT THROW ANYTHING AWAY!*** I made the mistake of taking notes and after a few years, thinking they were no longer important, I threw them away one day while I was cleaning. I would later realize they were important when we went to trial for malpractice; the opposing counsel asked me to recall the questions I had asked about the surgery and wanted a copy. I could not reproduce those notes nor could I prove that I asked any questions.

You can keep hand-written notes or put them in the computer. Include dates, phone numbers, the name of the person you spoke with, and what was decided.

Recording people's names with any conversation is important because people change jobs and the person you speak with today may not be there in a year. Your documents may be the only proof you have for your case. For example, create a simple chart like this:

What about research?

Become informed about all medical conditions or medical recommendations made to you. Do not just take the doctor's words at face value. Ours told us, "We will use the best product and make you 90 percent better." That did not happen.

The more questions you can ask, the more prepared you will be for your surgical procedures or treatment. I never thought to ask any of these questions before Dennis's injury. Even as a healthcare provider, I would not have thought to ask any of these questions of another physician. Specific questions to ask your practitioner or surgeon include:

- How will the procedure be performed?

- What is the name of the product you are using?

- Who manufactures the product you plan on using?

- How many times have you used the product?

- Is the product FDA approved?

- Will there be any drug company representatives in the operating room?

- Who else will be in the operating room?

- How long will I be in the hospital?

- What hospital will I be at? Then look up the statistics about the hospital.

- How long does recovery typically take?

- What sort of after-treatment (PT, OT) will I need?

Even if your doctor provides you with names of previous patients to talk with, that really doesn't mean anything. In our case, the surgeon did not use the same product on previous patients. So even though the procedure was the same, the product used was not even close! The product used for the patients we were talking to was Infuse®. The product that was used in our case was Trinity Matrix®. We were not comparing apples to apples.

According to Beth Israel Deaconess Hospital, spinal fusions require a 3.4 day stay and that has been consistent in their study from 2009-2011.

(Source: Spinal Fusion Surgery Volumes & Outcomes, 2012)

When we took Dr. Jones to court, the fact that the doctor provided names of people for us to talk to is made a big impact on the jury. What doctor gives patients names for others to talk to about their operation? In our case, the jury never heard the entire story and was making decisions with the information they had. I might have thought the same thing.

9. No Second Surgery!

While we were dealing with all the medical issues and Dennis's pain, we were also having challenges with the worker's compensation insurance company. Our attorney was fighting to have the medical bills paid and to receive weekly paychecks to make up for Dennis's inability to work. Dennis's unemployment payments were about to run out, and worker's compensation still felt it did not have to pay.

Our worker's compensation hearing was scheduled four weeks before the one-year anniversary date of the injury. Finally, two days prior to the hearing, our attorney called to inform us that the worker's compensation attorney had offered a settlement. It was a miracle! They agreed to give us back pay to the date of his injury, start sending regular weekly paychecks, and the medical bills were going to be paid. I stood there in disbelief, not knowing what to say or ask.

When such things happen, you are so grateful and in such shock, it is difficult to wrap your brain around what you are being told. All this information comes at you so fast. The attorney knows what is going on; he is familiar with the terminology and understands the situation. Sometimes, attorneys forget that all this is new information to those of us who are not experts in this field.

We were so grateful for the settlement and it could not have come at a better time. Our savings were dwindling and I could no longer afford the COBRA insurance. The settlement was one of the best gifts we have ever received.

It took three to four weeks before we received the check for a year's worth of back pay. When worker's compensation insurance pays your back pay, it comes in a lump sum and in Wisconsin, is not considered taxable income. We could finally pay our bills and replenish some of our savings. Things were looking up for us—or so we thought.

FUNCTIONAL CAPACITY

The functional capacity evaluation was the next medical injustice we underwent. A functional capacity evaluation is a test done by an objective party to determine a worker's level of disability. Our surgeon ordered the evaluation. It was performed by a physical therapist who would determine if Dennis was fit to return to work and if so, at what level, or capacity.

Dennis was put through a battery of exercises to determine how much he could lift, as well as how often he could bend, twist, sit, or crawl. Dennis and I went to the evaluation together and I watched the physical therapist perform the exam; I was not about to let my husband go through this alone.

WHENEVER YOU GET A PHONE CALL FROM YOUR ATTORY

Get as much information from the attorney as you possibly can and write everything down. You can ask your attorney to repeat things for clarity. Once there is time to digest this information, talk to others out loud about what you are being told. Make a list of questions that come up, then call your attorney for any explanations you might need. Ask if it's a good time for you to talk. If your attorney says no, then ask to set up a time to talk as soon as possible. Remember, you have hired the attorney, so he or she works for you, and can also be fired by you.

If you have a loved one going through such tests, never let that person go alone. Document everything you see! If I had this to do over again, I would take pictures or better yet, use a video camera to document this test. If you are the injured worker yourself, have someone accompany you to any doctor or therapy visits to document the exam.

The surgeon told us having this exam would help determine Dennis's level of disability. We felt this might finally provide some closure to this nightmare and help the worker's compensation insurance company determine his permanent restrictions.

We both knew he would never be able to do maintenance work again. He could not get on the floor easily, so kneeling and crawling were problems; it often took Dennis five minutes to get up and down from the floor. Even though it was difficult for him, he would try from time to time, figuring that if he did this, eventually he would be able to regain his strength and flexibility again.

The functional capacity assessment is supposed to be objective. Little did we know that going through the exam would create more issues with our surgeon. When we went to the surgeon's office to receive the results, they were presented in a brief, five-minute conversation. Little did we know those test results would determine our future. I remember the day like it was yesterday.

The surgeon held up the results and said, "Here are your permanent restrictions. I have good news and bad. First, the good news: you can work eight hours a day. The bad news is that you are unable to return to the maintenance work you did before." We just sat there, stunned. We could not believe what we were hearing.

There was no way the results the surgeon was holding in his hands correctly portrayed what had happened during testing. I had witnessed the exam and what physical activities Dennis was able to do.

The surgeon proceeded to tell Dennis that he should sit down and think about what he wanted to do with his life. We were not able to ask questions in the short time allotted to us. Then the surgeon turned to us and said, "If you are not interested in additional surgery, it's not financially feasible for me to continue to see you just to prescribe pain medication." Then he handed us a prescription for pain meds and told us he would refill the script for six months. After that, we would have to get them from someone else.

Can you believe it? Not financially feasible to care for us! That, after we had just paid him $90,000 for surgery! If we had ever wondered if medicine was a business, there was no wondering anymore

Every time I pointed out to the doctor that Dennis was getting worse, not better, and was far from the healing plateau, we were just blown off. We were told it takes a complete year after surgery before one reaches a complete healing capacity. We had been told that for the past six months, so how could Dennis be "fired" as a patient?

I looked at Dennis in disbelief. I thought this nightmare could not get worse. Here was a physician who had been good to us for the past six months. He was only one who had actually helped us when everyone else said there was nothing wrong. He found answers for us. Now he was kicking us to the curb with constant pain, no relief in sight, and no future assistance except surgical options. To add insult to injury, he was also telling us that Dennis could work eight hours again—without addressing the issue that he had no reflexes in his legs!

We were dismissed. Once again, our lives had been turned upside down. Not only had Dennis been laid off work, betrayed by his friend and employer, but Dennis's injury had also caused major tension within our family, since Dennis's brother still worked for the company. The worker's compensation insurance company was trying to get away without paying its share. The original doctors accused him of faking and now the only doctor who had treated us well and apparently believed us was turning us out without any kind of support!

On the way out to the parking lot, I began to read the report for the first time, trying to figure out what had just happened. The results stated that Dennis could kneel and crawl on the floor. I had been right there during the capacity examination; Dennis had expressed concern to me that he screwed things up because he refused to kneel and crawl. I was looking at test results that showed he had done these activities. Something was really wrong here!

When I asked him if he crawled at the appointment, he said, "I never crawled, I can't crawl on the ground!" Dennis was devastated. He looked at me sadly and said, "How can I go back to work like this?"

Our next challenge was trying to figure out how Dennis was supposed to return to an eight-hour workday when he was only sleeping two to three hours a night. His pain was so bad that he was using narcotics during the day to help relieve his symptoms and still walked with a limp. How would he drive under the influence of narcotics? How could he operate heavy machinery while using pain medication? There were so many questions running through my head at that moment.

Dennis looked at me and said, "Maybe I am just a baby. Obviously, everyone is telling me I am fine."

I figured I would be proactive and take care of this situation—I would just call and talk directly to the surgeon and he would understand my concerns. I called the surgeon the next day and expressed my concerns to the physician's assistant. He assured me he would talk to the surgeon and get back to me.

Then I decided to call the physical therapist who had conducted the exam to express my concern with him about the test results. My intention was to get information, not to make the PT angry or defensive. I know sometimes patients can get mixed up so I suggested this to him. After all, Dennis had refused to kneel and crawl. The physical therapist insisted that Dennis had been unable to kneel, but was able to crawl.

I replied "I was present for the exam and Dennis told me during the exam that he had refused to crawl."

The physical therapist began losing patience with me, and told me that Dennis had actually crawled ten feet across the room.

I repeated back to the therapist, "He crawled ten feet?"

His reply "That is correct."

Now I was really confused. How can someone crawl if he can't even kneel? I questioned this and was told that is what happened. The PT became agitated and told me he could not change anything in the report, and my only recourse would be to talk to the surgeon and have him change it.

I called and left several messages for the surgeon. I felt like I was getting the run-around from everyone. After two days of calling, I finally had the surgeon paged because he refused to call me back. When I finally reached him, I explained the situation. The surgeon became irate and began yelling at me, stating that this should not be his problem. He wanted to know why he was being called, "because the fucking physical therapist could not do his job properly." He began to tell me he was late to an event with his children and he could not deal with this situation at the moment, and then hung up on me.

After that horrible conversation, it took me several minutes to gather my composure. I never had another discussion with this doctor about the test results or anything else.

You may be wondering why having the extent of Dennis's disability corrected mattered so much. When the capacity test was done, it resulted in a change in payment from the worker's compensation insurance company. Because the report stated that Dennis could work eight hours a day, he would no longer receive total disability benefits. Instead, he would now receive permanent partial disability benefits.

My husband was still injured, still in severe pain, wondering how he was going to work eight hours a day, and what type of work he was going to perform.

DISABILITY AMOUNTS

Worker's compensation benefits are paid when the worker is found to have partial temporary disability, partial permanent disability, and full temporary and permanent disability. Every body part is assessed a percentage for partial and full disability. Payments are paid out in weeks based on permanent or temporary disability.

Information on rates for injuries and body parts can be found at www.ssa.gov/policy/docs/ssb

Our attorney told us the way around this incorrect report was to file a request for Dennis to return to work. If his employer did not respond, it meant the company was unwilling to take him back to work with his restrictions. The company did just that: no reply. Not only had Dennis lost his physical abilities, but his employer was now rejecting him as well. It was Dennis's worst fear coming true.

How could I let this happen to my husband? What type of doctor would I be if I let my own husband be sent back to work in pain, with nerve damage that no one recognized, and without training of any kind for a new position? I would have failed him and failed my family. There was no way I could fail everyone. There was no way I would give up the fight for my family.

It was difficult to get any of the doctors or physical therapists to understand that Dennis was not getting better. He was still in pain and could not bend or crawl on the ground. I was not sure what they were looking at when they examined him, because even I could tell he was struggling with his ability to move freely and he was in severe pain. I was at my wit's end! I had the knowledge, the training, and the medical background, but no one wanted to listen to my concerns.

I was scared for my husband and angry with the doctors. I also felt that I was an incompetent doctor. If I was having those experiences, I can only imagine how someone without a medical background must feel when they or a loved one is ill and the person is not getting the care that they need from their healthcare provider. Despite my training, I am really no different than anyone else; my medical specialty is not spinal injuries. I am at the mercy of the specialists, like all others. After many nights of crying, I knew we had to take a different approach.

So Many Questions

Once the decision was made to not proceed with a second surgery and Dennis reached the six-month healing plateau, the relationship between the orthopedic surgeon and us changed almost immediately. We were shocked and never saw the reversal coming.

Suddenly, the orthopedic surgeon was not friendly when we came to the office; he was short and to the point. He did not do an exam with the visits. One day, during our office visit, the surgeon said there was nothing else he could do for us. It was six months after surgery, Dennis was still not better; he actually was getting worse. He had not slept through the night in over 18 months, suffered increased pain, and had more difficulty walking.

How could this be? What would we do now? Would this ever get better?

We had these and so many other questions and were not sure what the answers were going to be. I was running out of ideas and resources within my medical community. I needed to trust someone else.

10. WOULD A SECOND SURGERY BE DIFFERENT?

I knew I needed to find one person in the medical field who knew what was going on and could provide some options to help my husband. I knew Dennis was not healthy and would not survive in his current medical and mental state. This was not a situation where Dennis would die from his injury, but I was not sure he could emotionally withstand the pain and the lack of ability to do all the things he used to do, like work, ride a motorcycle, and hunt. I called a trusted colleague and explained the situation once again. He told me there is only one person he would see in such a situation!

Immediately, I picked up the phone and called the recommended surgeon, whose office was 90 minutes from our home. When I asked to schedule an appointment, I was told Dr. Smith would not accept patients unless they had been out of surgery for at least 12 months. Dennis was only six months out. I sat on the phone in silence for what felt like a lifetime. I expressed to the secretary that Dr. Smith was my last hope.

I was in tears and with a broken voice, I asked, "What do I do?" I explained the situation: my husband was still injured and in terrible pain, unable to sleep, and walked with a limp. The previous surgeon had sworn at me when I questioned him about the functional capacity exam and even hung up on me. He had previously told us it was not financially feasible for him to continue to see Dennis and sent us back to our family practice doctor.

I think the secretary felt sorry for me, because she told me that Dr. Smith was not available for a few hours because he was in surgery, but she would talk with him and call me back. I was so grateful that she was willing to do this. I was desperate and told her if he could not help me, I was not sure what I would do.

By the end of the day, she called me back and told me the surgeon was willing to meet with us. Not only would Dr. Smith meet with us, he wanted to see us right away! We were scheduled for an appointment four days later. I was not expecting much from this appointment because of the way we had been treated by the other doctors and therapists over the past year and a half but I certainly was hopeful. Nevertheless, having Dennis's symptoms, pain, lack of reflexes, and inability to kneel or crawl completely dismissed, I was cautious.

Dennis was not sure about seeing another doctor. He was convinced no one would be able to help him again. He was having a hard time trusting anyone again. One doctor had already hurt him both physically and emotionally. Could another surgeon really help him?

* * * * *

When we arrived for our visit, Dr. Smith's office staff was wonderful; they were pleasant and helpful. The doctor spent 90 minutes with us during that first visit. After reviewing the MRI reports, CT scans, Diskogram reports, injection reports, and surgical reports, he evaluated Dennis. At one point during the exam, Dr. Smith looked at me and said the reflexes were absent in Dennis's legs. I wanted to cry from relief. I had been telling any medical people we had seen over the past 12 months and had been ignored. Finally, someone acknowledged my concerns. Dr. Smith asked if Dennis had ever gone through a nerve conduction test. I told him no. Dr. Smith was surprised that such an exam had not been performed, particularly given Dennis's lack of feeling in his legs.

From there, the story gets even more interesting. Dr. Smith told us the surgeon who had performed the first surgery—yes, the one who had sworn at me—had once worked for our new surgeon. Dr. Smith began to tell us that Dr. Jones was a hot head. The conversation proceeded and Dr. Smith explained that Dr. Jones was good at simple surgical procedures. Unfortunately, in cases like ours, Dr. Jones would not be the best choice. Dr. Smith told us they had worked together and were partners when Dr. Jones came to town. He was very familiar with Dr. Jones' surgical abilities and personality.

Dr. Smith also informed us that when injuries or surgeries do not heal the way Dr. Jones wants them to, he typically abandons the patient. I was surprised to hear this from this new surgeon. There is an unspoken code of ethics with doctors; they normally do not disclose issues about one other to patients. I was happy he was honest with us; I would like to think it was because I was a provider as well, but I now believe there was a bigger issue behind revealing this information.

I never did find out what it was, but have some ideas. Things were starting to make sense finally—that is exactly how Dr. Jones had treated us: he had gotten rid of us as fast as he could when Dennis's body was not responding the way he expected. Learning such things about Dr. Jones certainly made us angry, but when Dr. Smith proceeded to tell us the reason the first surgery was not healing—the hospital where the first surgery had been performed requires surgeons to use bone grafts made of an inferior product—I was furious! Nor have that hospital's surgeons stood up to the hospital on behalf of their patients and demanded the best bone graft material possible.

I could not believe what I was hearing! Nor could poor Dennis.

Dr. Smith then suggested that we speak with an attorney and gave us the number of someone he had worked with before. Since when does one physician turn against another? Such a thing is unheard of!

I am not naïve. I work in an integrative medicine field, and have heard hundreds of horror stories about our traditional medical system. But this was happening in my town, to my husband, and perpetrated by one of the largest healthcare organizations in our state.

Here is the truth—the dark side—about the medical world: Once you are in a hospital, especially for surgery, there is no way to control what is happening to you nor is there any way you can truly know what is being done to you. Medicine is a business and businesses need to make money. The truth is that unless people are hurting or ill, hospitals and doctors do not make money. If hospitals do not make money, then they cannot provide the services we require. Hospitals may charge higher fees but they also have higher write-offs, which come from insurance companies. For example, the hospital might charge $32 for a blood draw, but insurance only allows $6. The only dollar amount that will be collected by the hospital from the patient's insurance carrier (if the patient is insured) is the $6.

In most cases, the hospital cannot bill the patient for the remaining balance of $26. This is just one example of how the insurance companies work to reduce their costs. Hospitals charge more because if they do not charge at least the minimum that is reimbursable, they will lose

---

AVOID HOSPITALS WHENEVER POSSIBLE

It is important to eat healthy, get at least eight hours of sleep a night, exercise daily, and use integrative approaches to care, such as massage, acupuncture, physical therapy, nutritional support, and even genetics to treat symptoms before they become a full-blown disease.

If you are feeling poorly, make sure you seek medical attention early from an Integrative Medical practitioner; this is a person who practices both Eastern and Western medicine. This will help you avoid going to the hospital.

The Joint Commission's Sentinel Event program states that the number of Wrong Site Surgeries reported has increased from 15 cases in 1998, to a total of 592 cases reported by June 30, 2007. (Source: Mulloy & Hughes., 2010)

HealthGrades reported that between 2007-2009, one out of nine hospital patients developed a hospital-acquired infection.

Archives of Internal Medicine "showed that sepsis and pneumonia caused by hospital-acquired infections killed 48,000 patients and ramped up healthcare costs by $8.1 billion in 2006 alone."
(Source: Mercola, 2011)

---

out on a small amount. We will talk about this is greater detail in another chapter.

We are completely at the mercy of our medical system. Unless Americans wake up and realize they have a role to play here and take back healthcare, situations like ours will continue to happen, and become even worse. As a naturopathic doctor, I believe that we should do whatever we can to avoid hospitals and maintain our health. Prevention is better than treating disease after the fact.

Dennis was now facing a second surgery because a hospital apparently dictated to its surgeons what products were to be used—simply for financial reasons. I thought I had done my homework: I had picked a supposedly good surgeon; I had checked him out for complaints with the medical board. I did not know he had difficulty handling complicated cases—like my husband's.

What I hadn't checked out was the Wisconsin circuit court (http://wcca.wicourts.gov) to see how many malpractice cases Dr. Jones had against him; I later found out that there were eight. That certainly would have made us think twice before letting him operate on Dennis.

Medical malpractice happens when someone is injured as result of his or her healthcare provider's actions or a side effect from a device or medication that induce serious side effects.

Checking the state board of licensing, asking the correct questions, or being a provider myself, did not protect Dennis from becoming a victim of medical malpractice. We found out that Dr. Jones used an inferior product (Trinity Matrix®) that had not been FDA-approved in his surgery. In addition, he had used a stem cell that had never undergone any human clinical trials; the only animal trial conducted was done with one rat. Once the information was gained about stem cells and surgery, we were prepared to begin our discussions with the pharmaceutical companies. Having never been part of a lawsuit before, we did not know what to expect.

* * * * *

I cannot begin to convey how guilty I felt about the whole situation. My husband underwent an operation that would never heal properly based on my recommendation of a surgeon. Dr. Smith, surgeon number two, told us that he would likely not have done that operation in the first place. It was entirely my fault that Dennis would now have to undergo another surgery because of the permanent nerve damage that had been missed by three other physicians.

I felt horrible because I felt like I should have known about the product and the surgeon. Dennis is such a loving man; he never blamed me for what was happening to him. The only way I could manage my anger and resentment was to dive into my spirituality and trust that somewhere something good would come out of this nightmare. I did not undergo any type of counseling, but would recommend it to others if they need someone to talk with. I was lucky and had a spiritual group that met monthly and they supported me.

Such guilt is very common amongst healthcare providers. We feel it is our job to care for our families' medical situations and we should know it all and assist in making the correct choices. When the outcome is not what is expected, as a healthcare provider, we feel as though we should have done more, known more, and prevented this from happening. It is very hard to deal with both physically and emotionally.

* * * * *

Dr. Smith explained that because the first operation to fuse Dennis's spine had been performed by going through his abdomen, the only option to repair this fusion would be to make an incision through his back. Surgery had to be postponed until the results of the nerve conduction study were in.

Once again, Dennis and I were off to see another doctor for another procedure. He was going to have an EMG, or electromyography. This test involved placing needles along his back and legs, and then energizing them with an electrical current to see if the charges could stimulate any nerve reactions. It is not a test a person would sign up for unless it was absolutely necessary, especially for a man who hates needles. This test is torture!

Since Dennis was determined to get better, he did just about anything the doctors told him to, but trust me, he was not happy. Once again, I accompanied him to this exam. If you or a loved one need to get this test, my advice is to find a really good doctor who specializes in Physical Medicine and Rehabilitation (PM&R) or neurology to perform this test; otherwise it can be extremely painful.

When the first needle was placed and the electrical current turned on, the doctor was a little surprised: there was no reaction from the nerves in the lower half of Dennis's body. The doctor placed another needle and applied higher current and still no reaction. At that point, the doctor told us that the situation did not look good. He proceeded to place several more needles and apply current; none of them triggered the reactions necessary to confirm healthy nerve function.

Once the results of the nerve conduction test were in Dr. Smith's hands, he told us we had no choice: another surgical procedure was necessary and should be done as soon as possible.

Christmas was only three weeks away and we needed to decide how quickly the surgery should be scheduled. Dennis decided he wanted to have the operation before the holidays. My husband had dealt with the pain, the discomfort, the limp, and all the other complications long enough and just wanted to get the operation over with. It was his decision. I was worried that he would not be up to the holidays, but that wasn't a concern for him. He was pumped up and ready to get this done, so we scheduled surgery ten days before Christmas 2007, praying that God would give us the Christmas gift we were looking for.

* * * * *

Dennis's second surgery would be done at a different hospital. The incision would be made along his spine and they would take bone from his hip to do the graft. Using his own bone offered a better opportunity for healing and fusion, but would require an additional incision in the hip.

Every attempt would be made to clean up the nerves, but of course, there was no guarantee that the operation would help heal the nerves. These nerves had been irritated for so long all Dr. Smith could do was try. We were hopeful and scared at the same time.

Dennis would also need to wear a brace for at least two months after surgery to prevent him from moving or bending the wrong way. It would be similar to using a cast to help stabilize a broken bone in a leg or arm, and allow the spinal bones to fuse properly. The bolts and screws that were going to be placed in his spine were only there to hold the spine in place until the fusion was solid.

The explanation made perfect sense to me. At the same time, however, it made me question why the brace and bone graft taken from the hip had not been recommended for the first operation. Not only that, two weeks after his first surgery, Dr. Jones had told Dennis to "go ahead and do anything he wanted because he could not break anything or hurt it." I often question how much Dr. Jones's "advice" had to do with the failure of Dennis's back to heal, not to mention the use of an inferior product.

Let's review each graft individually so that you understand the benefits and risks of each of the grafts. Bone grafts are used by orthopedic and maxillofacial surgeons for the treatment of bridging non-unions of defects and reconstructions. An autogenous bone graft is osteogenic, which means it forms bone from living cells. Allografts are

> **MORE ABOUT BONE GRAFTS**
>
> There are four different types of bone grafts that can be used in surgeries.
>
> - Autogenous Bone Grafts
> - Bone Allograft Materials
> - Demineralised Bone Matrix
> - Bovine Collagen/ Hydroxyapatite Mixtures

an alternative, but these have low or no osteogenicity, increased immunogenicity, and resorbs more rapidly than autogenous bone. In clinical practice, fresh allografts are rarely used because of immune response and the risk of transmission of disease. Allografts can be helpful if a large amount of material is needed and it can be combined with other materials.

Demineralised Bone Matrix, also known as DBM, is commercially available and used in management of non-union of fractures. This is not suitable where structural support is required.

Bovine Collagen/Hydroxyapatite is marketed as a bone-graft substitute, which can be combined with bone marrow drawn from the site of the fracture. The type of material used in Dennis's surgery was the Demineralised Bone Matrix. (Source: Ben-Nissan, 2004)

* * * * *

The second surgery went off like a charm. I knew it had to because we had so many people praying for us. The surgery took three hours, a little longer than expected, but there was a great deal of nerve damage that needed to be "cleaned up," which meant that during the surgical procedure, they removed any debris or scar tissue that had developed around the nerves. After the procedure, Dr. Smith told us he had done the best he could, but he had never seen such "pissed-off nerves," meaning they were red and inflamed.

Now all we could do is keep our fingers crossed and pray. So we did!

This time, when Dennis awoke from surgery, he had no pain whatsoever. It was a miracle! By the second day, he was up walking and even climbing stairs with a walker. On the third day, he was able to go home after they removed a drain tube. He walked with a walker for about seven days, then a cane. His pain level was significantly less than before the operation and he was able to sleep. That alone was a huge success as far as we were concerned.

Christmas was only ten days later and he was able to attend our family gathering. With Christmas came hope and determination to heal. I believe we were given a Christmas miracle.

11. MEDICAL MALPRACTICE

Earlier I mentioned the word malpractice. I truly believe that is what occurred in our case.

According to the American Association of Justice, more than 98,000 people die from medical negligence every year in the United States. Medical negligence means a medical error was made. Fewer than one percent of such cases are reported to the appropriate medical board. Each state has a medical board that licenses and regulates medical doctors (MDs).

Most people do not seek the assistance of an attorney for compensation for their loss. People can sue for medical malpractice or negligence when harm is done as a result of a medical procedure or medical error. They can sue the hospital or the provider. Oftentimes both are listed in a case. Hospitals are responsible for their employees, which include nurses, doctors, technicians, and therapists—basically anyone employed by the hospital. In our legal system, the only way to make someone whole who has been injured by medical negligence is to sue for monetary compensation for the damages inflicted on them.

We so appreciated Dr. Smith explaining to us exactly what had happened during Dennis's first surgery with the recombinant bone graft and why it had failed. Such information is not typically disclosed to patients, for as I mentioned above, professionals generally protect other professionals: doctors protect doctors, policemen protect policemen, and so on.

When an injury like Dennis's happens, you blame yourself. Many thoughts flow through your mind: blame, guilt, anger—and worst of all, fear. Fear that you will never heal, never be pain-free, and never have your life back the way it was before the injury. You ask yourself: how did this happen? What could I have done to do avoid this? Why did I not see this was happening?

Later, thoughts about a new surgery enter your mind. Should you undergo another surgery? Is this the surgeon who can help you? Will he make you better? Can things get worse? What happens if this procedure fails?

Finding the answers to these questions and the hundreds of other ones that pop up is certainly not easy. I personally believe that no one ever really knows the answers, but if you follow your gut instinct, it will lead you to what the Universe has in store for you.

For the first time in 18 months, someone was telling us we were not crazy. For the first time, someone was telling us that the first procedure had not been done properly and had resulted in agony, sleepless nights, and the inability to work.

The ride home took an hour and a half in rush hour traffic. Dennis and I barely spoke two words to one another. When we actually started talking, many different things came out of our mouths and little made sense.

Dennis was not sure about a lawsuit and I have to say, I was not keen on that idea either. The physicians were still my colleagues and in the past, I had even been employed at the hospital that performed the original surgery. I personally would not want anyone to sue me for malpractice. What finally made us decide to take on the large hospital and the pharmaceutical company that marketed the bone graft product as equal to or superior to autologous (the patient's own bone material), was realizing that people were being lied to simply for financial reasons. We felt that we could not withhold this information, or sit back in good conscience and let others get hurt.

Several days later, Dennis and I agreed to at least call the attorney and start discussing the situation. There was nothing wrong with listening to what he had to say. That turned out to be the first step on a very long journey.

The attorney to whom we had been referred was extremely nice and very interested in our potential case. He provided me with a great deal of information about how product law worked, along with the reality of taking on a large hospital. It was not going to be an easy fight.

First, we had to prove that the bone graft product was inferior. We were going to do this by filming Dennis's second surgery to prove the material had not fused. The attorney wanted to show that after six months, the implantation of this bone graft was still soft. It was like silly putty in his spine.

Actually, this is the very first of many mishaps that occurred with the lawsuit. No filming took place but they did see the graft material was like putty. Because the filming did not take place, there was no proof to show at trial.

We also needed to locate the manufacturer of the recombinant bone product and if possible, get our hands on the product literature provided to the doctors. We wanted to know exactly how the product was being marketed to practitioners because we felt that they were conducting marketing fraud. Now you might think this would be easy, especially for a doctor like myself. However, nothing was farther from the truth. We began contacting the pharmaceutical company about three months after the first surgery for information, but we did not actually receive the information until after meeting with the attorney to discuss a malpractice case.

A few months after the first operation, Dennis had a massage. The therapist was worried about the heat radiating off his back where the surgery had been performed. In our world of alternative medicine, I thought that if I could get a sample of the material used, I could make a homeopathic remedy and use it to treat Dennis. I requested records to find the name of the pharmaceutical manufacturer, as I needed to know exactly what product was used and the name of the manufacturer. I called to explain what I wanted to do.

At that time, I should have realized something was wrong when the company representative told me it would not have the same lot number. When I explained that anything close would work in this situation, the representative was confused. The company was able to provide me with product information, but no actual bone graft material.

After being transferred to several other representatives, no one seemed able to provide me with the information I was looking for. After several months and multiple conversations with their legal department, I finally received product information.

I spent a Friday night reading through this information. What I found was unbelievable: the bone graft material used on Dennis was a product that had been harvested from cadaver bone! I could not believe what I was reading. Dennis and I had been told this product was synthetic; at no time was mention made that the graft material had been taken from a dead person's bones. This meant my husband could be at risk for hepatitis, HIV, and other illnesses that occur with human transplants.

Time to do my own research. First, I checked out the FDA website and began a literature search for product research and approval. This is a tedious and complicated task because of the plethora of information on this website.

What I found confirmed what we had been told by our second surgeon. The bone graft product used had only been approved for cervical spine (neck) grafts, not lumbar or low back, which is what Dennis had. It also appeared that the manufacturer was a German-based company. After more careful review, I discovered that the company had been started in Germany, but was now headquartered in the United States. The lawsuit would have been even more complicated if we had been dealing with a foreign company and foreign laws.

I thought the information I had discovered would provide good foundational material for our attorney. At our first meeting, we compared our notes and began to build a picture of what the bone graft manufacturer was up to. It was definitely marketing this product as one that was safe and could replace autogolaus bone (human bone) use. The reasons for using this product was to avoid having to make an additional incision to harvest a patient's own bone. This made no sense to me. Any time a person's own bone material can be used in this type of situation, it should be. Why would you want to risk infection and lack of healing just to save the person from another incision?

Dennis and I were also told that the hospital at which he had his first operation required the surgeons to use this product for cost-saving reasons. What actually happened was that the surgeon who performed Dennis's first operation was paid by the pharmaceutical company to help promote this product and act as a test site for the product. In return, he would be paid to assist them in creating new products.

During Dennis's first operation, the pharmaceutical representatives were in the operating room assisting and training our first surgeon on how to use the product. This is not unusual in new products. However, it should be disclosed in the informed consent process so the patient is aware of what is exactly being done and how. This part was never disclosed to us.

When I looked at our hospital bill, the insurance company had been billed for a different product so payment would cover the product. My research also showed that this particular product had never been approved for use in the United States at all! That was why the hospital needed to bill it under an FDA-approved product.

If the Food and Drug Administration does not approve a product for a particular use, it is considered experimental and health insurance will not cover the service or product. In my mind, this is medical fraud, but let me tell you it is not a big deal in the legal world. To my surprise, it becomes a small detail.

After discovering this, I went to our insurance handbook, which stated that the cadaver bone graft used in Dennis's first operation was experimental and therefore not covered.

When I contacted the insurance company to inform it about the fraud that had taken place, I was told it was too late to report it. It was now three years after the surgery. I asked about a preapproval that would have been done by the hospital or doctor's office to make sure the surgery would be paid by the insurance company. The customer service representative told me those documents were no longer available. This surprised me, because most documents pertaining to medical records are supposed to be kept for ten years. I think the customer service person really went out of his way to help me with the knowledge he had, but it was more than he could access.

I was also told that if the insurance company tried to reverse the charges now, we would be responsible for payment. The customer service representative told me that this was not a large amount of money and the company would not be interested in trying to prove this medical billing fraud. I was shocked, since people talk about medical fraud costing this country millions of dollars a year. I thought this information would help our lawsuit and prove that the surgeon planned to use this product from the beginning, but our attorney felt it was not going to make a difference in the case at all.

It becomes clear in a medical legal case that information you may feel is important the attorney may not because of how he or she is planning to try the case. This can be very frustrating, but it is rare that you will change your attorney's mind unless you find something really powerful..

WHAT YOU THINK IS IMPORTANT DURING A MALPRACTICE TRIAL MAY NOT MATTER

Did you know that around 73 percent of medical malpractice cases are won by the defendant, the doctor? This is according to a 2001 study conducted by the Bureau of Justice Statistics. During the discovery phase of a trial, many issues might come up that you, as the victim, feel are important, but which your attorney determines are not key to winning the case. As the victim, this is hard to swallow, because you want your story heard and you want justice.

There were many pieces we wanted aired. We had uncovered what appeared to be some illegal medical billing. I called our insurance company a little too late. By the time I thought to call them, four years had passed and the information needed for an insurance consultant to help me was no longer available in their system. It took several weeks and four phone calls for the insurance company to uncover the bills from the doctor; the insurance company was never were able to retrieve the entire hospital bill. The insurance consultant spent over two hours with me discussing the billing that was done; he could not find anything that showed there was any fraudulent billing that occurred. Needless to say, I was frustrated that I could not prove what I knew to be true.

I continued to search the Internet for information regarding the insurance code that would correlate with the exact fusion product Dr. Jones had used. I did find that in 2007, our insurance carrier had declared the product used in Dennis's surgery as experimental. That was enough to convince me that billing fraud had been committed. If a product is experimental and a code is used for a covered product that is fraud. The question was proving it.

Another concern loomed: if I proved fraud, would we have to pay for the medical treatments ourselves? I certainly did not want that to happen because we were already in financial stress without Dennis's salary.

I relinquished my search temporarily, but I wanted to see the bill for myself. I contacted the attorney's office and asked for the hospital bill. After review, this proved I was correct: the bill showed that the product invoiced was human bone. According to the insurance consultant I had spoken with, nothing had raised a red flag when it reviewed the claim.

Now I thought I had found something that could prove fraud. When I spoke with our attorney's assistant and asked for the bill from the vascular surgeon, whom we were told would be part of the operation by Dr. Jones, she said she had never gotten one.

A vascular surgeon was needed because of the type of surgery Dennis was undergoing. When an anterior approach is taken (going in through the abdomen), a surgeon who specializes in veins is needed because the incision is being made close to the aorta, a major blood vessel, and the internal organs need to be moved out of the way to gain access to the spinal area.

Both the attorney's assistant and I were confused regarding the supposed vascular surgeon bill. The assistant told me she had brought this issue to our attorney's attention early on, and was under the impression that he did not want to fight the battle of medical billing fraud. I saw all of the pieces as part of the larger battle. I was frustrated because I knew what was right and what was wrong, but could not do very much about it.

I actually decided to make the call to the vascular surgeon for clarification on the bill. After several calls and several weeks, I finally received a call from the vascular surgeon's office and was told they needed to try to find the bill from 2007. I left several messages, never received any response, and have still not found out if there was a bill.

My own medical biller also did some research at my request about properly coding the surgical material. Perhaps the code might not be important at this point, but if we could find some clear violation, it might be helpful. If nothing else, it could prove that Dr. Jones planned to use the product without disclosing it to us. After all, our health insurance company would have had to preauthorize the surgery and he

Prior Authorization

Prior to major procedures, like Dennis's back surgery, insurance companies require "prior authorization." This means that the doctor's office sends information to the insurance company, detailing what is to be done, and the insurance company responds as to whether or not the procedure is a covered service.

The insurance company can declare all or part of a procedure not medically necessary, alternative, or experimental if it desires. If the insurance company does this, the doctor can proceed with the operation, but it may not be covered by health insurance. It is up to the patient to decide whether or not to proceed with the operation.

would have had to disclose the product he planned on using. I wanted information on what was preauthorized! To me, this would lock it in that he lied about another issue.

Other areas I thought were important, but our attorney did not feel were germane to the case, were whether or not the hospital was liable for supervising Dr. Jones and how he had handled the pharmaceutical representatives. I felt that, based on the hospital policy, the hospital and doctor should have disclosed to us in our written consent that the pharmaceutical representatives would be present during the surgery to assist the surgeon. Hospital policy states that if pharmaceutical representatives are going to present during a procedure, it is to be disclosed to the patient. We were never told that anyone other than the medical team was going to be present.

Our consent form had never actually been witnessed or dated. I thought that is what made a legal document legal, but apparently that didn't matter either. I would never sign another agreement without making sure everything was correctly executed.

Another issue I really wanted to have brought into the case was the pharmaceutical whistleblower. I wanted to subpoena her so she could testify about how the pharmaceutical company had provided kickbacks to Dr. Jones. She would also be able to testify that the cages used during the surgery were the wrong choice because there were too many holes in the cage and the material would never adhere. Our attorney did not feel her testimony would help our case. Nevertheless, I wanted her more than anything and fought several times to have her testify on our behalf.

The last issue I thought was a slam-dunk for our case was the apparent Federal Drug Administration (FDA) ruling on disclosure on off-label or unapproved products. As a practitioner, it had always been my belief that a patient should be informed if a product being used is off-label or it is not FDA-approved for use. I do this in my own practice every day.

There is no such ruling! I was appalled! I was pissed off! How could we healthcare practitioners not be required to disclose a drug, device, or biologic substance that has not been approved by the FDA or being used off-label?

When a drug is used in a different way then it was intended it is called off-label use. This means the medication or product has not been studied in that use.

My medical biller asked how a health insurance company could pay for the material if it is not disclosed. Wouldn't the patient want to know if he or she was going to have to pay for something out of pocket?

According to our attorney, none of this information mattered. Too much information would only confuse the jury and take us away from our original argument: lack of informed consent. In my opinion, these issues would play an important role in informed consent. What do I know? I was seriously beginning to question myself.

As a healthcare practitioner, I think it is a complete disservice not to provide all the options to a patient. Information should not be limited on the basis of payments from a pharmaceutical company or anyone else.

If and when you go to court, be aware that the defendant's attorney will claim you are submitting the claim for the money. He or she will try to disgrace you. Insurers, government officials, and business executives are quick to blame attorneys who they claim pursue injured workers and encourage them to run up big bills. In fact, the amount of money our attorney received was not making him rich, but without him, my husband would have never been able to get what was owed to him.

UNCOVERING MEDICAL FRAUD

That first meeting with the attorney was not exactly what we expected it to be. Initially the plan had been to file a product liability lawsuit against the distributor of the bone graft product; our intention was certainly not to start a medical malpractice case.

As we collected evidence to initiate the product liability lawsuit, the story unfolded in ways we never expected. The links to corruption were deeper than any of us could have ever considered.

We determined that the marketing company was committing marketing fraud in their materials used to sell to the doctors. The company had a manufacturer that produced the product and another firm that developed and produced the marketing materials for the product. The company claimed that the product was as effective as using a patient's own bone obtained from the patient's hip. The studies that were done actually showed it was less than 20 percent effective in growing bone. Bone from a patient's own hip has a 50 percent chance of creating a fusion.

The company also claimed that the product was FDA-approved for use. However, it was not approved for use in the lumbar spine.

At this point, our main objective was preventing the manufacturer from continuing to provide false information to doctors and their patients.

* * * * *

It would be several years into the lawsuit before the truth about the bone graft manufacturer came out. Despite my efforts to discover as much as I could about the manufacturer, which I readily shared with our attorney, he was not very forthcoming about how the case was going to be fought. Finally, four and a half years into the suit, he told us he did not feel we had a case that was worth much money.

Personal injury attorneys get paid when they win a case. The more money they win in a case, the more money they make. Dennis and I were shocked. By that point, we had read the depositions and could not believe our lawsuit was possibly without merit after what had been disclosed. We were concerned that if our attorney did not think the case was worth a lot of money, then how much effort had he indeed put into the case?

* * * * *

The first step in any legal case is getting depositions from all the parties involved. Our first deposition took place with attorneys from the pharmaceutical company that created the bone graft product, the marketing company, and the hospital's attorney. Our attorney was present to protect our interests. So there were four attorneys asking questions. The depositions were taken four years after Dennis's second surgery.

The questions begin with one attorney at a time asking questions of each witness. Questions were asked in a way that could be used against the person answering in a trial, as well as to determine what information each party has and how damaging it could be against the opponent.

As plaintiffs, we were not the only parties to go through the deposition process. Our attorney had the opportunity to depose key representatives from the pharmaceutical company, the marketing company, and the hospital. By the way, a court recorder recorded everything said. It was when Dr. Jones, surgeon #1, was deposed that our case changed from a product liability case to one of medical malpractice. Through the depositions, we found out several interesting things:

- The product had never been tested on anything other than a single athymic rat, a rat whose immune system was depleted.

- No clinical trials had been conducted on this product because the pharmaceutical company was not interested in spending the money.

- Dr. Jones, our first surgeon, admitted to being paid by the pharmaceutical company and never disclosed this to Dennis or myself. He stated it was for creating a new product.

- Dr. Jones admitted to making the decision for the product to be used during Dennis's surgery because he did not feel that Dennis was capable of making that decision.

- The marketing company, Blackstone Medical, admitted to creating marketing materials that showed equal effectiveness of their product to autograft.

- We found out that Dr. Jones was not well informed about the product or its use.

- Dr. Jones admitted that he knew the product was made from cadaver bone but never disclosed that to Dennis or me.

- Dr. Jones admitted to not personally consenting Dennis on the surgery, but he thought Dennis had completed the informed consent form.

- During the deposition, Dr. Jones clearly stated that it was he who made all the decisions to use the product and had not felt the need to tell my husband or me exactly what bone graft product was going to be used. He also took full responsibility for the decisions made regarding the operation.

To provide an example, I've provided some excerpts from Dr. Jones's deposition based on the transcripts with the doctor. Our attorney was the one asking the questions.

Q: "Doctor, were you ever told that the product you used was intended to be used as an extender?"

A: "No."

Q: "Had you been told this would you have used it in Dennis's surgery the way you did?"

A: "No."

Q: "Were you advised by the pharmaceutical company that the product should be mixed with local bone?"

A: "No."

Q: "Were you advised that the product was volume dependent?"

A: "Probably."

Q: Were you told that its efficacy was cell-concentration dependent?"

A: "No."

Q: "Were you told that the only clinical study that was underway determined that the product was not promoting bone growth?"

A: "No."

Q: "What was your understanding on the relative efficacy?"

A: "I don't recall."

Q: "Were you told that in addition to filling the cages with the product, you should also use some on top or around the cages?"

A: "I don't recall."

In cases where numerous discs are being fixed and there is not enough graft material to be obtained from a person's hip or spine, additional product is needed to fill the space. This is called an **extender.**

Q: "If you have been advised of that, would you have done that?"

A: "Yes."

Q: "Do you remember how much of the product you used?"

A: "No."

Q: "Did you provide Dennis with informed consent?"

A: "Yes."

Q: "When and how did you do that?"

A: "Pre-operative consultation and on the day of surgery via signed informed consent."

Q: "Here is the form that you represent is the consent to operate. Is this correct?"

A: "Yes."

Q: "Did you go over this form with him?"

A: "No."

Q: "Who did that?"

A: "My physician's assistant or a nurse."

Q: "This consent indicates that you will make an incision in the abdomen, remove the disc, insert the cages and hardware, then fill the cages with recombinant human bone morphogenic protein [bone graft material]. Correct?"

A: "Yes."

Q: "That's actually incorrect, isn't it? I mean, that's not the product that was used with Dennis, is it?"

A: "It is correct that I did not use recombinant human bone morphogenetic protein in Dennis."

Q: "Did you inform your physician assistant that you were not going to use this product"?

A: "I don't recall."

Q: " Did you inform the hospital that you would not be using this product?"

A: " I don't recall."

Q: "Do you know why this informed consent is incorrect?"

A: "The informed consent form is a boilerplate document that represents the most likely, most commonly performed procedure and the ingredients that we use."

The deposition goes on for twenty more pages. Here is a summary of what came next. Dr. Jones continued to admit that the pharmaceutical company never disclosed information to him about the proper use of the product, or at the very least, he did not recall receiving any such information. I find it extremely hard to believe that an orthopedic surgeon, or any physician, would not remember any of the specific details about the clinical trials, the efficacy, or the proper use of the product.

Dr. Jones then went on to admit that all these decisions were made without appropriate discussions with Dennis, because Dennis did not have the knowledge to make those decisions. He completely disregarded the knowledge that I, as a nurse practitioner, possessed to understand the process.

In addition, Dr. Jones admitted to being paid $500 an hour to work on the development of a new plate-and-screw product. This was not the plate system used in Dennis's surgery. In the course of the trial, we learned that this payment was part of a kickback scheme the pharmaceutical company used to get the doctors to use its products. According to our attorney, such payments are acceptable and common practice within the medical community.

However, such payments are against the law. The United States Congress in 1977 enacted a prohibition against the payment of kickbacks in any form. The Anti-Kickback Statute arose out of Congressional concern that payoffs to those who can influence healthcare decisions would result in goods and services being provided that are medically inappropriate, unnecessary, of poor quality, or even harmful to a vulnerable patient population.

Some other interesting questions asked by our attorney during the deposition include:

Q: "Do you know why there were four pharmaceutical representatives in the operating room with you?"

A: "No."

Q: You have no idea how or why they were in your operating room?

A: "No."

I have never known a surgeon who did not know exactly who was in the operating room and for what reason. Once again, we could not believe what we were hearing. Perhaps Dr. Jones had been instructed to respond to any inquiries with a simple "yes," "no," "I don't know," or "I don't recall." Gradually, the truth about the surgery came to the surface. When representatives from the pharmaceutical company were deposed, they clearly stated that the bone graft product had never been tested and was not FDA approved!

This information was only the tip of the iceberg of corruption. Our task was to prove the appalling situation and move forward to change it so it wouldn't occur with other patients.

Here are some specific questions and answers taken verbatim from the transcripts to illustrate the levels of corruption with which we were dealing. To provide some background, realize that researchers who work for pharmaceutical companies are often not privy to relevant information, which is deemed proprietary information. This protects the manufacturer from intellectual property theft. From my perspective, this is actually a good thing, because a company can spend millions of dollars on research and development, only to have another manufacturer steal that idea or result and profit from it.

Again, the following is a verbatim transcript of our attorney questioning the pharmaceutical company researchers.

> "The Medicare and Medicaid Patient Protection Act of 1987, as amended, 42 U.S.C. §1320a -7b (the "Anti-Kickback Statute"), provides for criminal penalties for certain acts impacting Medicare and state healthcare (e.g., Medicaid) reimbursable services. Enforcement actions have resulted in principals being liable for the acts of their agents. Of primary concern is the section of the statute that prohibits the offer or receipt of certain remuneration in return for referrals for or recommending purchase of supplies and services reimbursable under government healthcare programs." (Manning, 1996)

Q: "You understand that to the extent the product had been demineralized, it had been treated with hydrochloric acid."

A: "That's not quite true. The demineralized component, which is treated outside of the cells, is treated with hydrochloric acid as part of the demineralization process, but the entire product was not treated with hydrochloric acid."

Q: "What percent was subject to that part of the process"?

A: "Only that portion that was called a demineralized cortical component would have any hydrochloric acid treatment, which is the standard way. Bone is part of the process, standard process of demineralizing bone." (*This statement did not make sense to me when I heard it, or when I read it again.*)

Q: "What's the purpose of that process, to your understanding?"

A: "The purpose of demineralizing bone is to expose its proteins, and thus, its growth factors."

Q: "The demineralizing process kills the cells."

A: "Correct."

Q: "You understood that the product was derived from cadaver material?"

A: "Organ donors. Dead people."

Q: "Taken up to 72 hours after death?"

A: "Correct."

Q: "Do you know if the concentration of mesenchymal stem cells in bone decreases following the time of death?"

A: "I do not."

Q: "Do you know if any scientific studies were conducted by the company?"

A: "No. Not outside of the company itself."

Q: "Did you have any understanding as to how the concentration of mesenchymal stem cells varied within the product?"

A: "I knew that it was a minimum of a thousand. But it could vary between 200 and 300,000."

Q: "Did you have any understanding beyond that as to how the concentration would vary from lot to lot?"

A: "No."

Q: " Do you know whether any studies have been done to assess that possibility?"

A: "I know that currently studies are being conducted. There are studies using virtually millions of stem cells per cc to form bone. I have never seen anything that says you can have too many mesenchymal stem cells.'

Q: "What study are you referring to where they are currently using virtually millions of mesenchymal stem cells to promote bone growth?"

A: "I'm not sure I can tell you that, because these are FDA trials to which I have NDAs."

Q: "What is an NDA?"

A: "NDA. A non-disclosure agreement."

Q: "Is it true that prior to beginning sales, there were no clinical studies completed by the company?"

A: "Correct."

Q: "It was also the company's knowledge that there were no clinical trials conducted, correct?"

A: "Correct."

Q: "As I understand it, the contract between the manufacturing company and the distributing company states that it would be the distributor who would do the testing of the product and clinical testing. Correct?"

A: "Yes."

Q: "Do you know when the studies began?"

A: "I can't tell you the exact timing, but clinical studies were planned, yes."

Q: "Do you know when the distributor decided to start selling the product without having completed any clinical trials?"

A: "There was no requirement to do clinical testing, as with all allografts."

Allograft tissue comes from a donor of the same species as the recipient but is not genetically identical.

Q: "Was there a discussion of the fact it might be a good idea to find out whether the product was effective before it was sold?"

A: "Only based on the pre-clinical work."

Q: "Do you agree that the pre-clinical work undertaken with respect to the product before sales commenced was not scientifically valid work?"

A: "I do not believe that."

Q: "You think the studies included a statistically significant number of animals?"

A: "I don't know the numbers."

Q: "You don't? I mean, what were the pre-clinical studies? One was the athymic rat, correct?"

A: "Yes."

Q: "How many rats were the subject of the athymic rat study?"

A: "I don't know."

> *Athymic means that something living is lacking a thymus gland.*

Q: "Did you ever take a look at that?"

A: "I don't recall."

Q: "What was the control for that study?"

A: "I don't know."

Q: "Did you ever review what the control was?"

A: "I don't recall."

Q: "Were there statistical numbers in the study?"

A: "I don't recall."

Q: "Was a control used for that study?"

A: "I don't recall."

Q: "What clinical studies were initiated after the product went into sales?"

A: "We prospectively wanted to follow patients who had anterior cervical fusions, patients who had anterior lumbar fusions, and there was a group that wanted to compare the product to autograft in the same patient by alternating right and left sides in a posterolateral fusion model."

Q: "Did any of these studies have IRB or IDE approval before they began?"

A: "None of them had IDE approval because it wasn't required. They had IRB approval at the specific sites."

> IRB: Institutional Review Board.
>
> IDE: Investigational Device Exemption.

Q: "What was the site for the ACF study?"

A: "There were multiple sites."

Q: "Was that study completed?"

A: "No."

Q: "Why not?"

A: "There was a point in time when a question arose about who was going to pay for the certain aspects of the data that was being obtained?"

Q: "What was the control in that study?"

A: "These were not controlled studies."

Q: "Why weren't these controlled studies?"

A: "Because they were post-market studies, which are rarely controlled. There was also tons of historical data that could give us information on the fusion rates in that particular model using standard of practice allograft."

Q: "There was an anterior lumbar fusion study, how was that referred to you?

A: "I don't recall."

Q: "Do you recall approximately how many people participated in that study?"

A: "I don't believe we ever received any data on that study at all."

Q: "Do you know why that was discontinued?"

A: "Lack of performance by the surgeons."

Q: "Lack of performance in what respect?"

A: "The protocols, although they were prospective and non-IDEs, still required a fair amount of work: that is, enrolling the patients, consenting them, going through the IRB. When we initially vetted the sites that we wanted to use, one of the criteria was that they had a full-time research person to help with this added burden. It turns out that many of these sites didn't have such a person, although they claimed to. So it was just a logistical, operational thing. It just never got off the ground."

After several hours of deposition, we finally got some answers as to why the studies had not been conducted. These answers were revealed in an email written by the pharmaceutical company's paid doctor who was in charge of the research. It all came down to money, the millions of dollars it would cost to do proper and conclusive research.

Q: "Skipping down [the email], you state, lastly, based on the above, further research is needed on the product if we seriously want to generate a Level I paper for publication. Correct?"

A: "Correct."

Q: "Then you state, however, cost versus benefit of doing this with a post-market product would need to be determined."

A: "Correct."

Q: "What were the costs versus benefits factors at that point?"

A: "Basically there was no autograft—no allograft, sorry, that I understand was ever evaluated with a Level I paper that is a post-market IDE kind of study. Not one. So because this tissue form was felt, was shown to be safe, it had the biologic principles of autograft, that to spend $20-30 million on a post-market study was not reasonable."

As the depositions continued during the day with the representative of the pharmaceutical company, the conversation focused on FDA regulations. It was determined that the product would need a far more detailed description, or it would need to be regulated as a device instead of a living stem cell.

I read the depositions and thought they provided good information. The pharmaceutical company admitted that no studies had been conducted because of lack of money. The distributing company admitted it did not have all the information and that the manufacturer had withheld critical information from the distributor. The researchers admitted that they never tested the product for viability because they did not want to spend the money.

Dennis, our attorney, and I felt that these statements were in our favor. After these depositions, I thought, "This is great. We have it! Nevertheless, I continued my research, mostly using the Internet. What I found was amazing!

When Osiris, the stem cell manufacturer, purchased the product line from Blackstone, Blackstone became the distribution company for the product. Because of the nature of the work and marketing that had already been done by Blackstone, Osiris planned ahead for lawsuits that would come up in the future. In the buy-out, $50 million were placed in an escrow account to cover the indemnification of these suits.

I also found a federal court case against one of the pharmaceutical companies listed in our lawsuit. The information had been provided by a whistleblower who had worked for the company. The document claimed that the pharmaceutical company had knowingly persuaded hospitals and doctors to file fraudulent medical billing claims to Medicaid, Medicare, and Tricare.

Stem cells are mother cells that have the potential to become new cells in the body. In order for stem cells to multiply, a host is necessary, meaning there need to be live cells present to regenerate healthy tissue. If dead cells are used, those cells cannot regenerate healthy tissue.

Previously, I stated that I had tried to prove that Hospital #1 had billed us fraudulently. These court documents were behind my suspicions. Though I ultimately was not able to prove fraud in my case, I do think it occurred.

The statements were only the beginning of the allegations that would be made. I decided to call the whistleblower, and talk with her myself to see if she knew anything about our case. I tracked her down in Florida, where she lived, and we spoke for over an hour. She told me about the kickbacks that had been paid to doctors, who were paid for supposedly making new plates, screws, or other devices. Those "devices" merely served as an excuse to pay a substantial reward to the doctors who played along. The company also paid for trips to Las Vegas and showgirls, prostitutes, and vacations.

I could not believe my ears. Could it be that Dr. Jones was part of this kickback scheme? The whistleblower did not recognize his name, but that did not mean he was not part of it, she told me. Apparently, doctors all over the country were being bribed in this fashion by her former employer, Blackstone. (The whistleblower lost her job. As of this writing, the case is headed to the United States Supreme Court.)

After I hung up the phone, my first thought was, "We got him!" I immediately called our malpractice attorney to share this information with him. I emailed him the document from the court records and he was not impressed. I could not believe he was not interested. How could this evidence not help us prove that Dr. Jones was a fraud? He told me he was aware of the case. However, when we discussed the details, it was clear to me that he didn't have all the facts. Finally, he told me that because it occurred prior to the date Dennis was injured, it does not apply to our case.

The case I was referring to had been filed in federal court, but the dates in question in the law suit were before Dennis had his surgery. I had expected our attorney to investigate and find out if Dr. Jones had been part of the kickback scheme. Quickly, I discovered that investigating for a trial in real life was not as it is portrayed on TV.

I was not going to give up, though, and tracked down another attorney, one from the South who had taken on Blackstone in the past. He was wonderful and spent over an hour talking to me about Blackstone and his experiences trying a case against the company. He confirmed what Ms. Hutchinson, the whistleblower, had told me about Blackstone and warned that if we pursued the fraud angle, we would need to be smart to win our case. The southern attorney was willing to talk with our attorney about what had worked for him and what our attorney should stay away from during the trial.

We were on the right track! Now we had someone who had fought this battle before and won!

After that conversation, I immediately contacted our attorney and gave him the name and number of the attorney who was willing to coach him. Our attorney told me his strategy was already planned and he did not need any help. I could not believe he would not talk with the third attorney. My trust in our own attorney was waning by the day. He told me that case had nothing to do with our case and that going off in this direction now made no sense. More importantly, we had one shot at this and he did not want to lose. He assumed if we won the case, it would be appealed and that would be his opportunity to try our case in the Supreme Court.

Our attorney told us several times he thought this case would end up in the Supreme Court because of its uniqueness based on the medical consent, or lack thereof. That was where we were headed. By this time and all these excuses, I was fed up with all these egos! I reminded our malpractice attorney that he worked for us and demanded that he call the attorney from Arkansas with whom I had spoken. Our malpractice attorney told me he would and then never did, which I found out after I called the attorney back who had given me the information about Blackstone. I begged him to help us with our case and consider taking on the case himself. It was just too late. We were only days away from mediation and a few months away from our trial date.

Part of me could understand our malpractice attorney's decision not to change his strategy a few weeks before mediation, but I also could not imagine going into a procedure of such magnitude without having this vital information.

Increasingly, I wondered if our malpractice attorney was the best attorney for our case. I began calling around to see what it took to change attorneys.

Let me tell you, if you are thinking about changing attorneys mid-case, don't bother. When you sign a contract with an attorney, you are in for the long haul. You need to read your contract, which outlines the percentage the attorney will receive if you switch. In our case, our malpractice attorney would receive 40 percent of the awarded money (should we win), and the new attorney would also need to be paid.

Our malpractice attorney was also ready to fire me, I think. When I told him we needed someone else, he told me, "Fine. Go ahead and find someone else." He knew that no other attorney within the area would take on this case so soon to mediation, nor is it common for one attorney to take another attorney's case. We couldn't drop the case at this point, either. If we were going to win, lose, or draw, we would have to stick with the malpractice attorney we had.

THE 2013 LAS VEGAS CONFERENCE

This story just continues to follow me around in ways I never expect it to. Slowly but surely, the pieces continue to fall into place.

I was attending our annual International Anti-Aging conference in December of 2013. I have attended such conferences for years, but have previously avoided any session discussing stem cells because of what happened to Dennis. At this conference, however, I decided to participate and learn something new about stem cells.

The lecture I happened to attend was presented by an orthopedic surgeon, who was explaining the use of mesenchymal stem cells (MSCs) MSCs and how they will never grow bone without a carry product. I was shocked that this was the topic of discussion, which involved how to use the MSCs so they can grow tissue.

After the lecture, I approached the surgeon with a question about solely using cadaver bone in an L5-S1 back surgery. He gave me a funny look and said, "We have known for years that it would never work." I thanked him and asked for his business card.

Later that night, a colleague of mine with whom I was attending the conference made arrangements for us to have dinner with a stem cell storage company. I was most definitely intrigued.

At dinner, I sat next to a gentleman who was a scientist for the storage company. Once we began talking, he told me that he had worked for Osiris Therapeutics. I felt like I was being sent a message. My colleague asked the scientist if we could talk with him about Osiris.

"Sure, I don't work there anymore," he said easily.

I began to ask him questions about the product and what so-called testing had been done. In all fairness, the man had left Osiris in 2003, and Dennis's surgery was in 2006, so some time had passed. With what I was about to hear, it didn't matter.

Let's call the scientist Cal, not his real name to protect his identity. Cal began to tell us that when he worked for Osiris, they had made a stem cell that would have grown anything. It was amazing. However, a new manager was hired and the process used to grow the stem cell media was altered. It changed the product, which was no longer considered superior, nor was it able to grow tissue. In part, this was due to the fact that restrictions on the age of the stem cells had been lifted. It no longer mattered how old the stem cells were when harvested. The company also modified the length of time between harvesting.

Cal also confirmed that no studies had been conducted on this product. He continued to tell me that the functionality of this product was no longer the same because of the modified media.

That was just the surface of our conversation. Cal asked how Dennis could have obtained the product. I explained that we had been told the surgeon was being trained in its use. Amazed, Cal stated that was impossible because the product had not been approved for use in humans. It should only have been used if Dennis had been part of a study. Dennis had never been part of any sort of study, nor would he have consented to be part of one.

I could not believe what I was hearing. Cal confirmed my discoveries when I had done research on the product four years prior.

Those two hours of dinner conversation helped me realize how much the company and the surgeon had gotten away with. How could a jury have expected me to know all this when the deceit and corruption ran so deep?

12. THE GIFT OF LIFE

The gift of life—organ donation—is the most beautiful donation anyone can make from the loss of a loved one. About two years before Dennis's work-related accident, my father passed away from a stroke. Our family made the decision to donate my father's tissue, ligaments, bone, and tendons to the local tissue bank.

The tissue bank was one of the first callers after our father's death, within hours of the death of our loved one. They are allowed to do this through public law 98-507, put in place by President Clinton in 1998. The law states that blood banks are *required* to call within hours of a death to request if tissue donation is desired. This was done as a means to obtain more organ donations and assist in saving the lives of those waiting for organs. While our father's organs (heart, liver, kidneys, and so on) could not be used to save a life, since he had died of stroke and had not been placed on life support, his other tissues could be donated to help raise quality of someone else's life.

My dad was the type of man who would have done anything for anyone. He had been raised in a small town where everyone helped everyone. When the call from the tissue bank came in a little after midnight the day my father died—October 18, 2005—we did not hesitate to donate his tissues. We were told that he could help many people with this donation. A family friend who was with us that night mentioned that she had been grateful for a tissue donation. Her son had been the recipient of a tendon donated several years earlier, and as a result, can walk normally at the age of 21.

For several years thereafter, we received letters about the people my dad helped with his gift of life. We laughed when we saw that in

2007, his bones had been given to six people who underwent lumbar fusion procedures, the same operation Dennis had suffered through.

Could it be that the gift from my dad had also gone to Dennis? We wondered about that for a few years. My dad had been a jokester, and after his own surgery, Dennis went through some experiences only my dad would have found funny, because he too had suffered with a bad back. We were able to find the humor in such moments, and it gave us some comfort thinking that maybe a small part of my dad had been reborn in my husband.

INSIDE THE TISSUE BANK INDUSTRY—MORE DECEIT

It was October of 2005 when Americans learned that thousands of patients throughout the country had received illegally harvested and sold tissue, ligaments, bone, and other body parts from a group operating under the name Biomedical Tissue Services of New Jersey.

These unlawfully obtained and distributed tissues had not been properly processed or harvested within the critical twenty-four hour time after death. Nor had the tissues been screened for infectious diseases, placing donation recipients at risk of HIV, hepatitis B, hepatitis C, syphilis, and other communicable diseases.

I stumbled across this information one evening while watching *American Greed* and saw the names of pharmaceutical companies scroll across the screen. Among them was the name of the pharmaceutical company and the product that had been used in Dennis's surgery. I could not believe what I was hearing. A once-reputable oral surgeon divulged that he could make more money selling cadaver tissue to tissue bank companies than pursuing his ethical work.

A single body being donated to provide tissue, tendon, ligaments, and corneas could yield between $140,000 and $220,000. Donating tissues is supposed to be a gift, not a for-profit operation. I learned that many tissue banks are for-profit operations. Selling body parts has become so profitable that people have been imprisoned for body snatching.

A combination of anger and anxiety flooded my entire body. I could barely move. How could someone who had taken the oath of "do no harm" put unsuspecting, innocent people at risk because of money. I was appalled, to say the least. When I could finally process what I was hearing, I began to wonder if Dennis had been a victim of receiving tainted tissue?

Once again, I pulled out my laptop and looked up the story online. Fortunately, this incident had occurred prior to Dennis's surgery and the FDA was aware of the situation. The FDA also informed all those who had received the tainted tissue so they could be monitored and followed for potential diseases.

To this day, I still am not 100 percent certain that the tissue Dennis received was completely cleansed and processed in the manner that was necessary to prevent spread of disease. It is my belief that as a doctor, it would have been our first surgeon Dr. Jones's responsibility to inform Dennis that he would be using a cadaver-based product and explain exactly what potential risks that decision might hold.

Dennis and I were never told that a cadaver-based product would be used in his spine, but instead, were assured that recombinant synthetic bone would be used. When we heard the word "synthetic," we would never have thought that would mean synthesized from dead bones.

We did not explore the issue of using cadavers to harvest bone tissue until 2011, when I uncovered the deceit and corruption inside the tissue banks. The "gift of life" is actually a money mill!

TISSUE DONATION AND THE MALPRACTICE TRIAL

During our malpractice trial, a great deal of information was brought up regarding the quality and effectiveness of the product itself. It was never mentioned that the product used in Dennis's surgery was a cadaver-based product. I thought this was an important piece of information that a jury should know about. However, our attorney did not agree.

The lack of clinical studies for the product was brought up; the jurors did not find this to be significant information.

I have since begun to research where my father's tissue has been sent and to whom his remains may have been sold. I truly hope to find that his body was donated as we intended. Needless to say, after uncovering all the other layers of corruption, I would not be surprised to find that his body had been sold. As of this writing, I still have not uncovered any information about what happened with my father's tissue.

It would be reasonable to assume that if you were getting a tissue sample, it would be from one person, but in our case, we found that bone tissue from multiple donors was commonly used. I gained knowledge on this from the Blackstone Medical marketing information and was reminded by the *American Greed* program. This meant that the graft material used for Dennis's back could be comprised of bone product from an 18-year-old or an 80-year-old. Older bone tissue does not have the same potential for regeneration as a younger, more vital bone product would. This would have been important information to make an informed decision to proceed with the surgery.

AMERICAN GREED FINDINGS

Death certificates of the deceased were forged and it was possible that patients received tissues from cadavers who had cancer, osteoporosis, HIV, or other conditions that might pose potential problems for these recipients. For example, the death certificate of *Masterpiece Theater*'s Alistair Cooke, who died at age 95 of lung cancer that had spread to his bones, was allegedly forged to state that he died at age 85 of a heart attack.

Of the 1,000 or more cadavers from which tissues were harvested illegally, most of the deceased or their family members had not provided consent to be tissue donors. Approximately thirty funeral homes have been accused of accepting money from Biomedical Tissue Services to ignore forged consent forms and falsified death certificates.

I would like to believe that a jury would also have found this information to be helpful and important had they been given the same opportunity to know what I know. Unfortunately, the information about cadaver-based bone product was never shared. Instead, the jury felt it was my fault that I had not been more involved in my husband's care and that I should have protected him. Nor did the jury feel that Dr. Jones, the surgeon who performed the first surgery, was at fault.

I am an intelligent woman. I have a Ph.D. and am a nurse practitioner. Could I really be so stupid and such a bad judge of character? Could our malpractice attorney not have seen it coming that I would be accused of writing false prescriptions? Dennis and I had not only been duped by Dr. Jones, gotten the run-around by the worker's compensation insurance company, and now were being hung out to dry by the legal system because our malpractice attorney was unable to prove his case. We felt like we had been duped by everyone involved.

13. Our Day in Court—The Trial

I t is difficult to explain what things are like in the courtroom until you have been there. Since neither Dennis nor I had been in a court setting before, we did not know what to expect, so I will share our experience with you through our eyes.

The first day of court trial begins with jury selection. I always thought that jury selection was just that. My understanding was that the attorneys would actually pick the twelve jurors, chosen from people who lived in the county in which the case had been filed.

In actuality, the process begins with a group of people who are requested by the county to serve their civic duty. Selection is made on the basis of driver's license registration. Many people are not interested in serving on a jury, and will use various excuses to withdraw from jury duty. Thankfully, there are people who do want to serve the judicial system.

> Jurors are selected on a random basis in the county that they live and the county that the case is being tried in. They are then pooled together and called on to report to the courthouse where they can be questioned and they will be either dismissed or asked to serve on a trial.

The Trial—It was all about Informed Consent

The process begins with questions being asked by the attorneys and the judge to determine if there are conflicts of interest or bias to either party—in our case, Dr. Jones, the first surgeon, was the defendant and Dennis and I were the plaintiffs. The judge can eliminate any person from the jury who has a bias or conflict. If the judge does not remove the person from the jury, then it is up to either attorney to eliminate this person from the jury, depending on the person's perceived bias. Each attorney is only allowed to eliminate three jurors. The goal is to have a fair jury; each party's attorney tries to select people who will lean more toward his argument.

The jury is then made up of twelve jurors and two alternates. The alternates serve in case one of the other jurors is unable to complete his or her time on the panel. In our case, we had a very balanced jury. We were hoping to have people who were smokers or who were not against smokers. We were also looking for people who were not biased against medical cases. A third criterion was that the jurors did not have a problem with hunters. We got just that: a balance of people who were open to all these concepts. The jury was allowed to go home at night and they were asked not to discuss the case while it was active.

The actual court trial begins the day after jury selection, with opening arguments from both attorneys. This is really where you realize what is going to be argued on both sides. Our malpractice attorney began opening arguments with his plan to prove that Dr. Jones did not provide informed consent or give us information about all the medical options available to us in order for us to make a decision based on what a reasonable person would have chosen.

Then the opposing attorney gave his opening argument. We were shocked by what we heard, to say the least. He intended to show that my husband was responsible for the non-union of his surgery because he was a smoker. He also intended to prove that I provided narcotics to my husband at the same time as his surgeon without disclosing this information to the surgeon. The next item was that Dennis's work injury was the reason he had a failed fusion. The opposing attorney also accused Dennis of being nothing more than a slug who wanted to leach off the system because he had not even applied for a single job in four years!

Sitting there and listening to someone say horrible things about Dennis and me that were not true was downright miserable! I was furious about what was being said about us. Our attorney had never prepared us for the attack from the opposing attorney and we felt blindsided. I told our attorney that I never prescribed narcotics; he told me not to worry about what was being said for it was not important to the case. But it was important to my confidence and self-esteem, and to my reputation and the well-being of my practice.

After the opening remarks, the plaintiff's attorney called his first witness. We were the plaintiffs so it was our job to prove that Dr. Jones had done something wrong and therefore could be accused of malpractice because he did not obtain informed consent. The first witness was Dr. Jones, the surgeon who performed Dennis's first operation. He took the stand and the questioning began: what type of surgery, what had

---

INFORMED CONSENT

According to the American Medical Association, informed consent is more than having a patient sign a form. Medical consent is a communication process between the patient and the practitioner that results in the patient agreeing to undergo a specific medical intervention.

In the communications process the healthcare provider performing the treatment and/or procedure (not a delegated representative), should disclose and discuss with the patient:

- The patient's diagnosis
- The nature and purpose of a proposed treatment or procedure
- The risks and benefits of a proposed treatment or procedure
- Alternatives (regardless of their cost or the extent to which the treatment options are covered by health insurance)
- The risks and benefits of the alternative treatment or procedure
- The risks and benefits of not receiving or undergoing a treatment or procedure.

The patient is then given time to ask questions about the surgery.
(American Medical Association, 1995-2013)

---

been disclosed to the patient, and other related questions. Dr. Jones came off as arrogant and eagerly admitted that he had made the decisions regarding the operation for us. He felt we would not understand the dynamics of the bone-graft products he used, and therefore did not have to disclose those details to us.

The arguments began about who was at fault regarding the failed fusion—my husband or the surgeon. For three days, the opposing lawyer pounded home the fact that Dennis was a smoker and had not quit long enough to allow a fusion to occur. We all know smoking is bad, but by that point, it was like beating a dead horse. I never would have thought that ultimately, the smoking argument would resonate so much with the jurors. It is time that people stop blaming smokers for all their health problems. I am the first one to tell patients that they should not smoke, but smoking had nothing to do with Dennis getting injured, or the fact that the first surgeon used an inferior product and made a decision to use a product that was never tested. Nor did he even give Dennis an opportunity to chose.

The next expert for our side was Dr. Smith, our current surgeon, who explained that Dennis has permanent nerve damage because the plates that had been placed in his spine were rubbing back and forth across the nerves, destroying them with every turn. The lack of fusion had not been detected early enough. Therefore, when Dennis first saw Dr. Smith, it was evident that Dennis did not have reflexes in his lower extremities. Dr. Smith also reviewed a CT that showed the non-union with the first fusion. He stated that the non-union was partially due to the fact that an inferior bone graft product had been used, one that was only forty to fifty percent effective as best.

Opposing counsel then called expert witnesses to "prove" that because Dennis was a smoker, he was the reason for his own non-union. Each of the experts showed that there was a double risk of non-union, which actually means about ten to twenty percent reduction in the union for smokers. Smoking decreases oxygen in the body and slows the healing process causing decreased revascularization of the bone graft. They also tried to show that the risk on non-union is at least forty to fifty percent, which means if the product only is effective forty-fifty percent of the time used in Dennis's operation, there would be no chance that a fusion would take place.

Dr. Jones claimed it would have been unethical for him to perform Dennis's operation if he had still been smoking. A urine test should have been done to detect nicotine to determine whether or not Dennis was smoking at the time of surgery; if nicotine were found, then surgery would be cancelled. However, no urine test had been done! Opposing counsel tried to place blame our primary care physician for not performing the urine test, but the defendant's expert witness testified that in his surgeries where patients smoke, he orders the urine test himself and stated he felt it was his responsibility as the surgeon. We thought this might be a win for our side.

Then our attorney called up expert witnesses to testify about the bone graft product and what would be considered standard of care or "gold standard." The opposing counsel's expert testified that "gold standard" or the best option for such an operation is still bone taken from a person's hip or the upper spine. That sounded positive for our side. He also testified that he had learned not to use a new product for at least two years to determine whether or not complications arose from the new product. He did concur that smoking decreases a person's healing ability, but only between ten and twenty percent.

The majority of the arguments for the day involved smoking and its effects on the surgery. At that point, I think everyone was tired of hearing that smoking was the factor in the non-union. It was the only smoking gun, so to speak, that the opposition had up to that point.

The second day of the trial was not much different; it still involved testimony about product quality and smoking. The fact that Dr. Jones was being paid by the pharmaceutical company was never brought up.

Nor was there much discussion of informed consent. Though it was shown that Dr. Jones had reviewed with us the basic and commonly known issues of consent, such as the possibility of infection or even death, Dennis had not been given consent at the hospital. No one bothered to witness his signature or date his signed consent form. They claim this is just a boilerplate consent form that the hospital provides. The consent form had a product name on it but did not mention the bone graft product actually used. We waited to hear experts talk about what informed consent meant so the jury understood the responsibility a doctor has toward a patient. But it never came.

During my research, I found an article in the American Academy of Orthopaedic Surgeons (AAOS) journal. The AAOS believes that surgeons may prescribe or administer any legal form of medicine in the exercise of appropriate medical judgment for indication not in the approved or cleared labeling, they have the responsibility to be well informed about the product, to base its use on firm scientific rationale and on sound medical evidence, and to maintain awareness of the product's use and effects. Surgeons should appropriately counsel patients about the benefits and risks of the proposed treatment, and alternative treatments that might be available. In the case of an adverse event with an off-label use, surgeons can submit a report to the manufacturer and/or the FDA. Orthopaedic surgeons should disclose all conflicts of interest to patients, institutions, and medical associations and adhere to all state and federal laws and regulations. (B. Sonny Bal, 2012) None of this was done in our case.

The adequacy of any informed consent is dependent on state law. The majority of states employ a reasonable practitioner standard to assess the consent process, a standard that asks what a reasonable practitioner would have disclosed to the patient in similar circumstances. Physicians testifying as experts generally establish this standard. It becomes the responsibility of the attorney fighting the case to prove this process was not done.

Informed consent does not just tell you that an infection can occur or you can die. It is the doctor's responsibility to tell you what all your options are for treating your condition. You as a mature adult or guardian of a child have the right to make your own medical decision. To make that correct decision, you need to have all the information according to some of our higher medical agencies, the FDA, and our legal system. The doctor can decide what information he or she provides to you so that decision can be made.

Dennis and I were baffled by the fact that we were told our case was being fought based on informed consent and all we heard was a malpractice case. We consulted with our attorney and shared our concerns and questioned him. I asked him if it would help if we had an expert on informed consent. I proceeded to tell him no one had even defined "informed consent" yet. Our attorney just looked at me, nodded his head, and walked away. He never mentioned the topic again. We waited for more comments to be made about informed consent throughout the trial, but not a single expert was produced to discuss informed consent and no more information was provided to the jury about informed consent.

Finally it was our turn to take the stand. Our attorney was worried that we were going to take the stand and screw up the entire case. Since he never prepared us for the trial or to be witnesses, he could not be sure what we would say or how we would respond. When I requested a preparation day prior to the beginning of the trial, it was not at all what I expected. I thought the attorney or his staff would ask us questions and then provide us with advice on how to answer the opposing counsel At least that made the most sense to me, but on the preparation day, the only thing we were told was what to wear and how much make-up to put on. We were told that they would ask about how we met and what our relationship is like currently.

Because Dennis and I had never been prepared properly, in my mind at least, we were both very nervous when Dennis took the stand. Our attorney asked Dennis some basic questions: name, age, and what his work career was like before his injury. Dennis was nervous and had a difficult time answering the questions.

Then opposing counsel got his shot at us. Like a bull at a rodeo, he began attacking Dennis, stating that he had been injured at work and that his functional capacity exam proved he could work full-time. Our current surgeon had lowered Dennis's work restrictions based on a phone call from me. Despite the light-duty restrictions, Dennis had not

When someone is disabled and he or she cannot return to the job, the person is entitled to services through the state Department of Vocational Rehabilitation. This department provides the person with services to retrain him/her for a new position based on the person's limitations.

looked for a single job in four years. Dennis agreed with this because he had gone through retraining with the Department of Vocational Rehabilitation to open his own business as a taxidermist.

The opposing attorney began asking what Dennis had been told by Dr. Jones, the first surgeon, regarding the surgery. Dennis got very upset and confused the names of the bone graft products—the one that was supposed to be used and the one that was actually used.

Dennis's memory, particularly his short-term memory, has not been the same since that first operation. He has a difficult time remembering even the simplest things. Big win for the opposing side!

Then Dennis and the opposing attorney began to argue about smoking and the product that should have been used. Dennis told the attorney that a urine test had never been done and that he (Dennis) wanted to see the test! Then Dennis turned to the jury. He gave the example of building a house. If there is a contract that includes top-of-the-line windows, and the actual materials used are inferior, that means a breach of contract. Members of the jury nodded their heads in agreement. It was the first time anyone had been this blunt or direct throughout the two days of trail. Dennis thought he did a good job.

Then came the discussion about medication. The defendant's attorney asked Dennis if it was true that I prescribed narcotics. Dennis denied that. The attorney then asked if I had prescribed Ambien. Our attorney and I both stated that Ambien is not a narcotic—at the same time! The judge scolded me for talking in the background.

By that point, the environment in the courtroom was heated and everyone was upset. The judge decided the jury was tired and frustrated. He ended the proceedings for the day and sent everyone home. We were all grateful.

When Dennis came off the stand, our attorney and I told him that he had mixed up the two bone graft products. He was not even aware he had done so, and became so angry he just wanted to leave, rather than staying to confer with our attorney.

During that brief discussion, our attorney told us that he was glad we had gotten the settlement money from the pharmaceutical company. Apparently, that was his way of telling us we were losing. All of us were feeling defeated and upset. Dennis and I left for home.

Discussions circled around what had happened and we spent all evening preparing for the next day. We tried to understand what had occurred and how we might fix the damage that had been done.

We decided to call our attorney to plan for the next day. He had calmed down and so had we, at least a little. The plan was to bring Dennis back on the witness stand and keep any answers short and sweet. The attorney would bring up the original deposition from Dennis to show that Dennis had not known the product name. He had become confused from the two days of discussion during the trial.

When we entered the courtroom the next day, the judge immediately called the two attorneys into his chambers to talk with them about the case. We later learned that he had instructed them to stop fighting and get the case over with. The judge could tell the jury was frustrated with the fighting and wanted the trial to come to a conclusion. It was amazing to see how an argumentative opposing attorney can calm himself down when the judge tells him to do so.

Dennis was called back to the stand again. No mention was made about the prescriptions. The opposing attorney asked Dennis about his ability to hunt and fish; he showed pictures of us hunting and fishing from our daughter's Facebook page. Then he showed the jury a picture of us riding our Harley-Davidson at a Ride for the Cure breast cancer fundraiser. He used these images to show that if Dennis is able to ride a motorcycle, hunt, and fish, he should also be able to work. Then questioning was done.

No rebuttal from our attorney? We were shocked and dismayed at the unexpected turn of events.

Then it was my turn. I felt that I was now well prepared for any questions. If I had been called to the stand the day before, I would likely have been so flighty, I would have tried to protect Dennis and most likely ruined the case.

First, I was asked to describe how I met Dennis and tell the jury a little bit about myself. I was fourteen and Dennis was fifteen. It was love at first sight, except neither of us had the guts to tell each other. We later married at twenty-four and had two children. At the time of the trial, we had been married for twenty-one years.

I was then asked to describe the difference between nursing degrees for the jury. I began with a LPN, or licensed practical nurse, a one-year trained degree nurse. An RN, or registered nurse, undergoes two, three, or four years of training to become degreed, and typically works in a hospital or clinic. Then there is a certified nurse practitioner, which is the training I have. The judge then asked me to talk about what a nurse practitioner does. He was aware that nurse practitioners serve as primary healthcare providers within indigent or poorer communities.

The next line of questioning was about what I remembered being told about the surgery. Dr. Jones had stated that he would use recombinant synthetic bone. No one ever asked me what I understood that to mean. As a matter of fact, no one asked me if we had been given an option about the surgery or if we had just been told what would be done.

I felt that this distinction was important, but our attorney kept telling us it did not matter. At that point, I really still did not understand what was going on. How could none of this matter? How could it not matter that the surgeon was paid off? That we had not been given a choice? That the surgeon missed Dennis's non-union and the nerve damage that was occurring?

Our attorney rested the case.

Then it was time for the defendant, Dr. Jones, to tell his side of the case. The only witness the opposing attorney called was Dr. Jones, who got up on the stand and did a song and dance about how he had told us about all the risks of the surgery. He claimed he took us to a conference room and played a video to describe the operation that was going to take place. He claimed he told us that a vascular surgeon would be assisting, which was not the case. Dr. Jones also claimed he went over all the risks involved in the operation, and put on a demonstration for the jury that would have made anyone ill, parading around, pretending to be nervous. He shook and talked oddly, almost looking as if he were having a seizure. I believe he was trying to show the jury that he was a wonderful doctor. He was clearly trying to connect to them and talk to them on their level. By the time Dr. Jones was done testifying, he had the jury eating out of his hands. He was completely the opposite persona of the arrogant, self-centered man who had operated on Dennis.

After watching this amazing performance, I turned to Dennis. Neither of us could believe we had surgery done by this guy! I was ready for our attorney to blast Dr. Jones and reveal the true egotistical man inside. Our attorney asked only three questions, enough for Dr. Jones to admit that he had not given us options and that he decided to use the bone graft product without consulting us. Dennis and I looked at each other and I said, "I finally get it. He only needs Dr. Jones to admit that he did not give us options."

We were already planning to appeal whatever the decision was from the jury, so our attorney knew what he needed to do get the decision overturned at the appellate level. Dennis and I were feeling good about the trial thus far.

Then the defense rested its case. We were shocked. No other expert witnesses for the defense were called.

The jury was dismissed for lunch, and after they returned, would hear closing arguments. After that, the only thing left was deliberation.

We returned from lunch to hear that the judge was considering declaring a mistrial! After four long years, we are finally at court, and we may have a mistrial. Our attorney, Dennis, and I were stunned.

The judge came out of his chambers with a few legal books, citing cases of informed consent. He then asked Dr. Jones a question to determine if he felt the pharmaceutical company had provided him with enough information for him to make a decision on the use of the product. After conferring with his attorney, Dr. Jones confirmed that he had received enough information. Dr. Jones then made reference to my testimony: that Dr. Jones had told us he was using bone graft material and that was on the consent form.

The judge explained that this was therefore not a simple informed consent case. Neither side provided any experts on informed consent nor did the judge feel he should have objected to certain parts of testimony during the trial provided by the witness and other parts of the testimony should have been objected to that he did not. Therefore, he was declaring a mistrial.

The jury was brought out and told that based on a lack of information, the judge had declared a mistrial. Like us, the jury members were stunned. They sat there, just looking at each other, not understanding what had just happened. They were instructed that they would be dismissed and they were allowed to discuss the case with friends and the attorneys if they would like to, but they did have a choice and should not feel obligated.

We watched as Dr. Jones was whisked out quickly by his attorney to meet the jury so he could hear how great he was. He paraded in the hallway with the jury, who fawned around him. This was a perfect way for the opposing counsel to find out exactly what the jurors believed and what they didn't. I suspect this is the insurance company's attorney's way of seeing what he needs to change for the next go-around, if anything.

Dennis and I were so angry and disgusted with the entire system that we just wanted to go home. After a short conversation with our attorney about next steps, he felt that he understood where the judge was coming from.

We spent the next few hours talking about what happened. After the initial shock and anger, we were actually glad the judge declared a mistrial. We felt we had a fair judge who knew exactly what was going on and had made the best decision for us personally. He used an analogy that Dr. Jones had promised us diamonds and given us rocks. That was a good way of describing what happened.

Although we would have to go through a trial again, we would be far better prepared. Before all the parties left the courtroom that day, the next trial date was scheduled. The next court trial was scheduled for May 7, 2012, seven months away.

I immediately decided to do my own research so I could take a more active role in the case the next time around, which I had not done for the initial trial. I had been out of the loop for four years. I had let our attorney make all the decisions and not include us in on what was going on in order "to protect us." I would not fall for that excuse again. I had done research, but had let the attorney have total control on how the case would be fought. That is not like me. I am somewhat controlling in my personality, but I have learned that this is not a bad thing in cases like this. I made sure to tell our attorney to plan ahead and get ready for me to be a pain in the ass with questions and ideas on how to use information in this case.

If you find yourself in a trial situation, make sure you are in contact with your attorney as frequently as possible. If you can advocate for yourself or a loved one, you will understand the process better and may have good ideas that your attorney would not think of. You know the situation and what happened better than anyone. You may not know the laws or exactly how to put it all together, but with a little research, you can be a big help

BACK TO THE TISSUE BANK ISSUE

It was about a week after the mistrial was declared when my anger began to lift at least slightly. I could talk with my friend and medical biller for my own clinic, Isabella, about what happened in court. She was helping me review the medical bills for fraudulent billing. By that point, no acts of fraud would surprise me. We were also researching the cadaver product used during Dennis's surgery. That was the first time anyone asked if cadaver bone had been used. Where had the bone come from? What a novel question.

I had forgotten all about the *American Greed* show I had seen almost a year earlier, for I had been told it had nothing to do with our case. The incident shown on TV had happened before Dennis's surgery and therefore had no weight in our case at all.

Isabella asked the question again, "This company has to get the bone product from somewhere."

Thus the research began as she and I looked for the tissue bank that had supplied material to the pharmaceutical company. We found the tissue bank we thought might be associated with the manufacturer. What a beautiful explanation they had about how they used cadaver bone to make plates, screws, and implants for people who could not use their own bone material.

She then asked how the tissue bank charged for the bone, followed by "How can they sell tissue and bone to the pharmaceutical company if it's supposed to be a 'gift of life'?"

Isabella became a donor mom when her son died in a tragic accident. She had donated her son's body for transplant and the thought that her son's parts had been sold bothered her. She also volunteered at our local tissue bank, educating people about tissue donation. She was furious and hurt. We both wondered what was going on.

I also filed a consumer complaint with the FDA. Anyone can file a complaint with the FDA if he or she experiences an adverse effect from a medication or medical device. This can be filed on-line at www.fda.gov.com.

Twelve hours later, the woman I spoke with began by explaining the company that manufactured the cadaver product had registered the product as "bone graft" material. This means it is not registered for use directly in the spine or to be injected into the spine. I could not believe what I just heard because this product had been injected directly into Dennis's spine. She was disclosing the inferior product and the misuse of the product. The FDA determines the type of product registration based on the testing and research that is presented to them. Imagine my surprise upon hearing this news. How could Dr. Jones have used a product against FDA registration without disclosing this to us? Why wasn't Dennis allowed the opportunity to make an informed decision on this?

I was curious as to why our malpractice attorney hadn't made this call. Just a few days prior to the FDA call, our case against the pharmaceutical company was settled. Our attorney told us the only reason he thought the pharmaceutical company settled was because it was afraid of our FDA threat. Now I felt as though our malpractice attorney had sold us out as well.

Why was the FDA information first being uncovered now—and by me? It had been four years since Dennis's operation, and I thought every rock would have been turned over to win this case. Once again, my trust in the system was wavering.

My poor friend and colleague Isabella was in tears after what we had heard from the FDA—the manufacturer was purchasing cadaver bones from tissue banks and using them in its products. Her feelings about her son were running raw. All she could say was "I want my son back!" I could not blame her. I began to wonder where my dad was as well.

That same night, I feverishly began to research tissue bank fraud on-line. One would think by now I would no longer be surprised by what I uncovered, but of course, my emotions were running high once again. A small part of me hoped that not everything about our journey would uncover corruption. My stomach was empty and burning at this point. I continued to read the bold print.

TISSUE DONATION A $500 MILLION BUSINESS

Tonnie L. Katz wrote in an article in the *Orange County Register* from 2000:

"People who donate have no idea tissue is being processed into products that per gram or per ounce are in the price range of diamonds," said Arthur Caplan, a professor at the University of Pennsylvania's Center for Bioethics. The products enhance millions of lives, according to industry trade groups." Cadaver tendons help athletes return to the playing field. Slings crafted from human skin solve bladder troubles. Corneas prepared for implant allow the blind to see.

> About 20,000 dead Americans became part of this manufac-
> turing cycle in 1999, four times the number of bodies used for
> vital-organ transplants. The tissue trade now generates about
> $500 million annually.
>
> "There is a profit," said Michael Jeffries, chief financial officer
> for Osteotech Inc., a leader in the bone business. "It's not an
> evil thing because the profit is put to good use."
>
> The full article can be found at: www.sweetliberty.org/issues/
> hate/bodybrokers.htm

I could not believe what I was reading. What had happened to the word donation? The company mentioned here, Osteotech, was not the manufacturer of the product used in Dennis's surgery, but nonetheless, it supplied a great deal of product to the market.

What my research uncovered was that many orthopedic surgeons were asking for cadaver product because it would significantly benefit their patients for a variety of surgeries. Not only did they ask for more cadaver product, but many of them were also owners or shareholders in the for-profit tissue banks.

This should be a clear violation of the Stark Law. But it turns out these medical people are protected! The Stark Law was put in place to protect that patient from being referred to a facility owned by a physician or physician group. When doctors own a facility, as in the orthopedic groups and they own the tissue banks, this is an inside referral and violates the Stark Law.

The concept is to make tendons and ligaments available to help people walk and use their arms again, and supposedly, such products are usually only used in cases where it is not possible to harvest enough bone tissue from the person's own hip or spine. The cadaver product

THE STARK LAW

Physician self-referral is the practice of a physician referring a patient to a medical facility in which he has a financial interest, be it ownership, investment, or a structured compensation arrangement."
(Stark Law, 2008-2013)

used in my husband's surgery cost our insurance company $6,800, which does not seem like a donation to me. In addition, the cadaver bone product would never build bone without being mixed with human live bone, according to the FDA and three other expert witnesses, orthopedic surgeons who testified at our trial.

According to the California tissue banks, there are significant costs involved in harvesting and preparing such products itself. This information is found online. I highly doubt that 2 cubic centimeters of bone matrix cost $6,800 to process.

As I continued my research, I discovered that a human body donated to a tissue bank can yield the tissue company anywhere from $14,000 to $34,000 dollars for bone donations. If the person donates ligaments, tendons, and corneas, the sales price can go up to as much as $220,000. (Katz, 2000)

I remembered what I had seen on *American Greed*. The report was about an oral surgeon who was stealing body tissue and selling it to such tissue banks. He was getting rich from stealing bodies from the mortuary and falsifying the death certificates. The program showed that no care was taken to ensure the tissue was harvested within the critical 24-hour time frame to ensure that the tissue was still viable. Cells and tissue begins to die immediately after death, so procurement specialists have limited time to harvest tissue.

Worst of all, the oral surgeon did not care if the people from whom he harvested the tissue had died of diseases such as Hepatitis C, HIV, or cancer. The authorities caught him, but not before innocent people had been hurt by his greed. The FDA notified those involved, but that was after the fact. Only the oral surgeon and the mortuary were held responsible for the horrible crime. No mention was made of the tissue banks that had received the cadaver material. Did they not have any responsibility for the travesty?

If the profits for cadaver product were not so high, people would not be tempted to steal bodies.

We had donated my father's body to our local tissue bank and had never been told that his body would be sold to the Musculoskeletal

Transplant Foundation (MTF), which is a non-profit organization dedicated to providing allograft material. The tissue bank that harvested him perhaps made more money from selling his tissue than my dad made in a year. There is something wrong with this picture! MTF actually had a website where people can buy the type and amount of tissue on-line. I was appalled!

Should there not be some type of respect for our loved ones who are being given as a gift of life? Basically, tissue companies have become the middlemen, brokers for the sale of dead people's tissues. Tissue has become just another commodity.

I had no choice but to tell my mom what I had found out. Then I called Isabella to tell her as well. She has been a volunteer for our local tissue bank, assisting in recruiting tissue as a gift of life. She was speechless.

I cannot begin to understand how it must feel to lose a child. My dad's death was hard enough, but to feel that something good would come from the horrible death of your child, and to now feel like you had been completely taken advantage of was even more devastating! I cannot begin to imagine her pain.

THE NATIONAL ORGAN TRANSPLANT ACT (NOTA)

The National Organ Transplant Act of 1984 (NOTA) is the statutory charter of the United States transplantation system that bans the sale of body parts for use in transplantation.

The U.S. Congress banned profits from the sale of donated tissues in 1984. If selling tissue isn't profiting, I am not sure what is. To date, no one has challenged this 1984 ruling and no tissue bank has been prosecuted, at least that I could discover. Since then, Congress has tried to enact new rules, but has not succeeded yet. Rep. W. Bill Young recently made a request to amend the National Organ Transplant Act (NOTA) bill to prevent bone marrow and cord blood from being sold. Many of the non-profit tissue bank organizations have CEOs earning six-figure salaries.

Our local tissue bank is owned and operated by a non-profit hospital organization, which owns 80 percent the healthcare facilities in our state. They also own and run the blood center that oversees the tissue recovery center. To me, this seems like too much control and power for one organization.

There are four large, profit-making tissue banks in our country. According to Orange County Register, in 2000, they earned upwards of $142 million. I'm sure it's more now:

> The biggest deal in the industry was struck 13 years ago. Osteotech opened its doors in New Jersey without access to bodies. The company spent $10 million to start a nonprofit tissue bank serving as its exclusive broker of human bones. The publicly traded company is now the nation's largest producer of bone products.

> As for the tissue bank, The Musculoskeletal Transplant Foundation is the world's largest. The bank's chief executive, Bruce Stroever, predicts the industry will double to $1 billion by 2003. "Osteotech couldn't go it alone and had to invent us," said Stroever, who earns $350,000 a year running the nonprofit. "Neither one of us would be here without the other." In Florida, the opposite model occurred. The nonprofit University of Florida Tissue Bank spun off a private firm, Regeneration Technologies Inc., in 1998.

> *Orange County Register* (Katz, 2000)

How can this not be selling tissue for profit? As I write these words, I am filled with the deepest regret. I know my father's body helped people, but I was the one who encouraged my family to donate his tissue, skin, bone, and ligaments.

RECOMMENDATIONS FOR ORGAN / TISSUE DONATION

If you are interested in becoming an organ donor, I would recommend a few things:

- First, talk with your family so they know your wishes.

- Second, do some research on what happens to you and the organs should you decide to donate. Each organ donation requires something a bit different. For instance, if you do not want to be put on life support ("Do Not Resuscitate" order) , there will be a limitation on what organs you will be able to donate.

Once you have completed your homework and have decided you still would like to donate your organs, sign the back of your driver's license and get the orange dot to place on your card. This will let people know you are an organ donor in case of an accident.

14. WHAT HAPPENS AFTER A MISTRIAL

S ince Dennis and I had never been through anything like this before, we have absolutely no idea what to expect now that a mistrial has been declared. Our attorney told us that we would talk about our options in a few weeks. He had the settlement money from the pharmaceutical company in a trust and was collecting all the bills from the trial. He explained we would be getting a letter from him outlining what our options were at that time.

I remember the day I received his letter. I was at the office seeing patients. I dislike opening any letters from my attorneys during the day when I am seeing patients because it disrupts my thought process and usually stirs up feelings I have difficulty processing. I should have known better and avoided opening the letter, but I did it anyway.

As I read the letter, I could not believe what I was seeing. The attorney was taking 40 percent of the money and we would receive 30 percent, then the worker's compensation insurance company would get the remaining 30 percent. He then outlined a few other options on how to proceed.

During mediation, I had given up my option for consortium loss. Consortium loss is paid to the spouse for loss of their significant other's abilities, such as companionship. The attorney would go to the judge and ask for money to be set aside for consortium loss, which would give us a little more money. Our final option would be to retry the case and ask the judge to give us less than 20 percent of the settlement and the attorney would keep the rest for future expenses. The caveat is that we also received a letter from the opposing counsel and it threatened that if we go forward with another trial, they would come after us for taxable losses that would cost us between $7,500 and $15,000.

I was furious now. We would have to pay them!? Were they kidding? I immediately called our attorney to question him about this situation and discuss what we should do at this point. He could sense my anger and frustration and I made the comment, "So we will get nothing and you and worker's compensation will get everything."

He replied by saying, "I really can't deal with your anger today."

I was speechless for a few moments.

"My mother-in-law died last week and I am putting my son in rehab and I just cannot deal with any more anger."

I was still speechless.

"Give me until next week. I will be in a better place to deal with you. I know this is my issue and totally my issue."

What does one say at this point? It took everything I could to spit out the word, "Okay," and hang up. Furious does not even begin to describe how I felt! I could not believe it! It had happened to me again! The attorney's brush-off completely reminded me of the conversation with the surgeon when he told me to fuck off. This time, it had at least been polite.

I continued to see my patients for the rest of the day. Thank goodness, there were only two left. As my day ended, I went back to my computer to check email one last time. There was another email from the attorney, with two juror questionnaires attached. I opened them, holding my breath. I could have never been prepared for what I was about to read. Why would I again be surprised that I could be so hurt and shocked?

Both jurors blamed me for Dennis's situation. It is my fault that I had not been more involved with his care and I did not do enough research. I am in the profession and should have known exactly what was going on. They also felt that Dennis's ignorance was not an excuse for him not knowing what a doctor was going to do. I could not believe what I was reading. They both felt the smoking did play a role in his non-union. They both disliked our current surgeon and felt he was a joke! I could not believe my eyes. Were these people stupid?

I cried all the way home. All my guilt and feelings that the whole situation was my fault and the tribulations of the past four and half years were confirmed. I should have done more and should have protected my husband. How could I have known that these things would happen? How could I have known that the surgeon would be paid off and that he did not know anything about the product he was going to use?

I was so depressed I could not get out of bed for three days. I just sat and stared at the TV. My eyes filled with tears randomly throughout the day. I cried and wondered how I would recover from all of this.

After those three days, I roused myself enough to talk to another attorney, because by now, I was convinced we needed a new lawyer. This attorney explained what was going on and told me the case had been tried really well, at least from what I was telling him. By the end of our conversation, the attorney asked me if I was getting some help myself?

At first, I was offended but then I listened to how compassionate he was. He began to explain about how difficult it is for victims to go through a medical malpractice case. No one tells them that they will be accused of doing everything wrong and that it is their fault that this injury occurred. He was right! No one tells the injured person and his or her family how difficult and hurtful these times are.

I finally began to let go of the hurt and anger for a moment or two but it was not over. We needed to decide if we fight forward and try to win or should we just walk away with the small amount that we already had and go on with our lives and try to heal.

After many conversations, Dennis and I decided it was time to move on, let go, and live once again. We were both on the verge of emotional breakdowns with no sleep and all the anxiety and worry about how we would make it financially. It was time to just live and let go. So we did just that!

TOOLS FOR PROTECTING YOURSELF AND YOUR FAMILY

15. Navigating the Murky Waters of the Insurance Industry

Of course, this book would not be complete unless I gave you tools to help you navigate the insurance industry or the information to understand how this industry has become so powerful. The following chapters will provide you with the information needed to assist you with either your worker's compensation or medical malpractice case.

It has been thought for years that medical malpractice claims have caused insurance premiums to rise and courts to be overwhelmed with people looking to get wealthy off of the poor, innocent doctors who are only trying to help people.

Jurors have been a big help to the insurance industry because they are tired of people taking advantage of the system to get rich. As a result, 80 percent of the time, the jury will find in favor of the doctor as long as he just admits that he made a mistake, according to the American Association for Justice (AAJ) issue of medical negligence.

The insurance industry has taken advantage of the system and how people feel with tort reform. Tort reform refers to governmental—both state and federal—proposed changes in common law civil justice systems that would reduce tort litigation or damages.

Here are the facts regarding what is really going on with the insurance industry, based on a series from the American Association for Justice (AAJ) that highlights the issue of medical negligence. AAJ previously released: "Medical Negligence: A Primer for the Nation's Healthcare Debate," which examined some of the chief myths and facts surrounding medical malpractice, patient safety and access to healthcare. An article called "The Truth About Defensive Medicine," actually debunked claims that the threat of liability drives up the cost of healthcare; *The Insurance Hoax* analyzed the financial performance of the ten largest medical malpractice insurers in the United States, and; *Five Myths About Medical Negligence*, revealed the truth behind the biggest misconceptions about medical negligence. All of this information can be found at http://www.justice.org/medicalnegligence.

People opposed to comprehensive healthcare reform have used the current debate as an opportunity to discuss tort reform, in short, limiting the legal rights of injured patients. Those who are for tort reform believe it would reduce the amount of money insurance companies have to pay out to victims of medical negligence. As a result, this would lead to lower medical malpractice premiums for physicians, which, in turn, would lead to lower healthcare costs and health insurance premiums for all Americans. In *Five Myths about Medical Negligence*, you will see that this concept has not held true in states that have enacted restrictions on patients' rights, compared to states that have not. The primary sources of data are based on annual statements filed by the insurance companies themselves and data from the National Association of Insurance Commissioners (NAIC).

The truth is that states that have enacted caps on damages result in significantly increased insurance company profits. Medical malpractice insurance company profits have gone up in all states, but in states with caps, they have gone up even faster. Insurance company profits are 24 percent higher in states with caps even though they are paying out less and keep more.

Insurance company profits are happening ONLY due to caps on damages. These caps were supposed to lower physician premiums or healthcare premiums, but this has NOT happened. The only ones gaining, of course, are those in the insurance industry.

Medical negligence laws were passed under false pretenses. The medical malpractice insurance industry has seen a 47 percent increase in profitability in the last ten years. You will not be shocked when I tell you that overblown reported losses were used by the insurance industry to justify new measures restricting the rights of those injured by medical negligence.

Of course, it is the insurance companies that are enjoying extremely high levels of profits. "In 2008, the average profit of the ten largest medical malpractice insurers was higher than 99 percent of the Fortune 500 companies and 35 times higher than Fortune 500 average" (source: National Association of Insurance Commissioners).

The "medical malpractice crisis" has long since ended and is now quietly replaced by a period of extremely robust profits. It has gradually changed since 2003. Twelve states have enacted tort reform, bringing the total number of states with some form of cap on medical malpractice claims to more than thirty. We have not seen healthcare costs decrease. We have not seen patients' healthcare premiums decrease. We have seen medical malpractice insurers' profits go up dramatically.

This is another ploy by insurance companies to produce their own wealth. According to industry trade organization, the Insurance Information Institute (III), insurance companies' operating margins are the best in the last twenty years, surpassing even the boom years of the early and mid-1990s.

In 2007, medical malpractice insurers, based on insurance transactions alone, had profits of 25 percent. This amount was more than double than the entire industry, which was 11 percent, according to the National Association of Insurance Commissioners (NAIC). Clearly, medical malpractice insurance has proven even more profitable than the property/casualty insurance industry.

You can see why insurance companies have begun to fight so hard to win medical malpractice cases. They will continue this strategy as long as those profits keep rolling in.

WHAT IS BAD FAITH?

Insurance companies are required to "willingly" pay claims properly and promptly. This is known as "good faith." It is illegal for insurance companies to "willingly" not pay, discount, lowball, delay, or deny payment of legitimate claims in "bad faith."

When worker's compensation, personal medical, auto, or any type of insurance company decides to let claims go unpaid, it is considered bad faith. People are injured—from all involved: the worker/insured party to the insurance holder, the business owner. In this book, I am primarily focusing on worker's compensation, but the scenario is the same, regardless of the type of claim. The worker will end up getting an attorney, who will ultimately cost everyone more money.

Insurance companies that have practiced bad faith for decades have had years to rig Americans. Bad faith (BF) insurers choose do avoid making payment of claims, and unfortunately, other countries have also chosen to follow these practices. Research shows that about 85 to 95 percent of the insurance companies practice bad faith (BF) (Bad Faith organization, 1998-2012); they repeatedly and consistently break the law. It should be no surprise that there is a quiet, covert revolving door between the insurance industry workers and state regulators (Bad Faith Organization, 1998-2012). These are the people put in place to protect us from this type of practice. Yet, you guessed it—they are getting paid off to keep quiet and turn a blind eye. This contributes to the status quo of claims resolutions.

According to www.badfaithinsurance.org, here are the top ten insurance companies known to practice bad faith:

- State Farm
- Hartford
- Allstate
- Unum
- Cigna Health
- Berkshire Hathaway
- CAN
- Assurant
- Ace Re
- American Family

HOW DO YOU KNOW IF YOU ARE A VICTIM OF A
BAD FAITH CLAIM?

First, has your insurance company refused to pay your claim without a valid reason? This goes for any type of claim, even traditional medical insurance. Insurance companies have contracts with doctors to pay a set rate. As a patient, you will get an explanation of benefits known as an "Explanation of Benefits," also known as EOB, which provides an itemized statement of exactly what your doctor charged, what the insurance company has paid, and what you are responsible to pay. It also shows the amount the doctor must write off as part of his or her contract. You should get familiar with reading this so it makes sense and you will know if the insurance is paying according to the contracted amount.

You should understand that there are different contracted rates with providers who are "in-network" or "out-network." If providers are in-network, that means they agreed to receive a discounted payment for services. In return, they will have access to a larger number of patients. Providers who are out-network have not signed a contract with a particular insurance carrier. Therefore, they do not accept discounted payments. As a patient, you have the choice of seeing any provider in or out of network, but be prepared to pay a higher co-pay or co-insurance if you are seeing a provider out of network.

Providers who are not contracted with insurance can choose to be out of network. It does not mean that they are not good providers. It means they have decided to provide care to patients without being dictated to or limiting the care that is provided. You should know if you are seeing a provider who is in-network or out-network before your appointment so you can make a decision to take on the added expenses.

Bad faith insurance companies will play many games in order to get out of paying a bill. They will first request records, then find a small detail that they will say is experimental or alternative. This allows them to deny your claim—not just that part of the claim, but the entire claim. They will also fail to promptly and thoroughly investigate a claim; unreasonably delay payment; unreasonably deny benefits to a claim;

unreasonably interpret the translation of policy language; and refuse to settle the case or reimburse you for the entirety of your loss.

If you think you are a victim of bad faith, contact your insurance company and try to correct the problem. If that does not work, contact your state insurance commissioner and file a complaint. Remember that your insurance policy is between you and your insurance company, not between you and your healthcare provider.

To prove bad faith, you only need to show that the insurer failed to honor the contract and had no cause not to pay what was due. Now that sounds easy, right? Well, not so easy because you have to prove it in court. For more information on how to manage a bad faith claim, go to www.badfaithinsurance.org, which provides all the information needed to assist you.

16. FIGHTING WORKER'S COMPENSATION FRAUD ON ALL FRONTS

The following material is compiled from a variety of sources, including the California Department of Insurance, Alameda County District Attorney's Office, and from the James Bond Investigations.

All the players in the worker's compensation arena can commit fraud. Each player commits fraud for the same reason: MONEY!

Fraud is everywhere in business these days. People are looking to get rich quick. I will tell you that there is no get-rich-quick scheme when you have a situation where business owners, doctors, lawyers, and chiropractors are involved in organized crime and ripping off the system. Workers fake injuries. Companies choose not to report the nature or the number of their workers, whose jobs are an important factor in determining how much the employer pays. For instance, it's not unusual to see a roofing company pay premiums for one roofer and 30 secretaries.

In recent years, the insurance industry's focus on cheaters and malingerers has helped push through national worker's compensation reform, a profitable cost-cutting campaign supported by outrage over alleged abuse of the system. The problem, however, is that the fraud image is false for the vast majority of worker's compensation cases.

Studies show that only 1 to 2 percent of worker's compensation claims are fraudulent, according to the California Department of Insurance. Certainly, the tens of thousands of workers killed or injured every year were hardly aiming for a free ride on their employer's tab.

The fraud that is committed makes it difficult for all those involved in worker's compensation to receive a fair evaluation, including the attorneys and the insurance companies. It would be beneficial to all involved if people played by the rules. However, that does not seem like it will happen any time soon unless there is some type of reform in the worker's compensation system.

There are ways around a worker's compensation claim and fraud seems to be a big player in this arena. There are red flags that would alert a person that someone might be committing fraud. Here are the definitions of fraud for all those involved and the red flags that should make you think that someone may be committing fraud.

Attorney fraud arises when attorneys knowingly participate and misrepresent the truth to either secure or deny compensation for their clients or themselves. Examples: knowingly assisting a client in pursuing a false claim, knowingly pursuing collection of a lien the attorney knows is fraudulent, related criminal acts such as paying doctors, vendors, or others for referral of clients or settlement of cases. Also suspicious: if the majority of claims are of a questionable nature or several workers from the same employer have reported similar injuries and are represented by the same law firm.

Insurance adjuster fraud occurs when a claim adjuster purposely misrepresents the truth in order to either deny or support a claim, or offers any form of consideration for a settlement of a claim. Examples: Adjusters accept gifts from doctor's offices in exchange for implied promise of patient referrals. Adjusters knowingly refer cases for rehabilitation services that are not needed in exchange for a rebate or other monetary gain. Lastly, adjusters may alter evidence in a claim in order to support a denial of a claim.

Of concern are also include inconsistent application of cost-containment measures or agreement to pay above the fee schedule, increased use of a particular vendor that would lead to excluding others, or vendors outside the preapproved panel being used. Adjusters who have social relationships with an applicant's doctors or attorneys are a concern or adjuster's lifestyle grossly exceeds their apparent income.

Employer fraud: There are two different types of **employer fraud** in worker's compensation. One is claim-related and involves policy premiums. The second type of fraud occurs when an employer knowingly misrepresents the truth in order to deny or obtain compensation of behalf of workers, knowingly lies about entitlement of benefits to discourage an injured worker from pursuing a claim.

Employer premium fraud occurs when an employer knowingly lies in order to obtain a worker's compensation insurance policy at less than the proper rate.

Examples: If an employer misrepresents the risk or exposure for an insured by under-reporting payroll, misclassifying payroll, and reporting an injury. Employers may lie about the injury and claim by saying it happened at home instead of at work. They may lie to the worker and tell the worker that he or she would not be covered for six months. Some employers will offer to pay the worker's salary while they are off work, along with medical bills, to avoid having the injury go through worker's compensation insurance.

Worker fraud. We cannot forget that workers may commit fraud as well. This happens when a worker lies about becoming injured on the job to collect money and receive time off from work. Examples: A worker gets injured at home but waits until he goes to work and then pretends to fall or pretends to lift something wrong so he can claim it on worker's compensation.

The following are examples that would indicate further investigation for potential fraud is needed:

- The injured worker is a new hire.

- The applicant takes excessive time off prior to the claimed injury.

- The injury occurs prior to or just after a strike, layoff, plant closure, job termination, or completion of temporary work. For example, a claim for injury occurs immediately after a disciplinary action, notice of probation, or demotion.

These do not automatically mean a person is guilty, but they are certainly indicators of potential fraud. These red flags should be followed up on when appropriate. To prove criminal fraud, certain questions need to be answered, such as: What is a lie? Was the lie intentional? Was the lie made to purposefully deny benefits or delay them? If you think fraud is a factor in your case, discuss this with your attorney.

17. FILING A MEDICAL MALPRACTICE CASE

If you believe you have been caused harm at the hands of the medical profession, the first step is to know if you have a case at all. You will need a third-party doctor to review the case to see if there is merit to your situation. It may be easier to contact an attorney to discuss the details of the case. He or she will have contacts to help to review your information. After you have reviewed your case with an attorney and it is determined that medical malpractice is likely, a civil case will be filed.

You want an attorney who specializes in medical malpractice and has a track record for winning! Many attorneys practice personal injury, but there are specific skills to fighting a medical malpractice case. The money involved in fighting a case like this can be several hundred thousand dollars.

Once the case is filed, all parties involved will be notified: doctors, nurses, hospitals, and their insurance companies. Then the discovery process begins. Information will be gathered to prepare the case and depositions will be taken from all parties.

A civil trial date will be set usually a few weeks before the trial settlement negotiations begin because a trial is so costly for both parties. If the defense does not want to settle and the plaintiff's attorney feels that the claim can be successful at trial, then some will make it to a courtroom.

To prove negligence and win a malpractice case, there are four basic legal elements required: duty, negligence, injury, and causation.

There is a statue of limitations for filing for your case. This time limit varies depending on what state you live in. It is important to talk with an attorney as quickly as you can after your injury so you do not miss the statute of limitations. If you miss it, you will not be able to file your case. Many states have exceptions for minors, reproductive injuries, or objects left inside a person.

I mentioned this earlier but will say it again because it is so important: *interview more than one attorney.* Ask many questions, such as:

- What is your success rate in settlement negotiations?

- How often do you go to trial?

- How many malpractice cases have you had?

- What type of knowledge does the attorney have about your medical situation?

- Pay particular attention to the attorney's attitude when speaking with you. Is the person engaged and listening or does the attorney seem distracted and put off by what you are saying? You should connect with your attorney and feel like you are able to communicate with him or her about anything.

LEGAL ELEMENTS OF MALPRACTICE

- Legal duty means that the defendant owed you legal duty under certain circumstances or under the law.

- Negligence in a medical malpractice case is that the doctor did not provide you with standard of care or breached their duty to you as a patient.

- Injury means that they caused harm to you.

- Causation is an easy-to-answer question: If it weren't for the act of your doctor, would you have been injured?

If you hire an attorney and it does not work out, get out of the relationship as quickly as you can. Read through your contract carefully before you sign it. Make sure you understand exactly what you will be responsible for at the end of the trial. How much will you have to pay your attorney if you win or lose? You want to know what you owe the attorney if you decide to fire him or her. Some attorneys place a clause in the contract that states if you fire the attorney, you will still owe the attorney's percentage, plus you will owe the new attorney his or her percentage. That means you will get less and the attorneys will get more.

All the information discovered belongs to you, not the attorney. If you decide to leave your current attorney, ask for all the discovery materials. They will have to forward this information to your new attorney. You do not want to have to pay for discovery again; that can be costly and set your trial back.

Do not expect a medical malpractice case to be over quickly. Most medical malpractice cases are not settled for many years. Some people who are seriously injured die before their cases make it to trial. Even if you win your case, it is common for the opposing party to appeal the decision. This could end up taking an additional two years or more and if your case ends up at the Supreme Court level, you can expect an additional four to five years before a settlement is reached.

The stress of preparing for a trial takes a toll on the family, personally and financially. It is important to find ways to manage your stress during this time. Managing stress when you are ill or in pain means you need to build a support system. Find something that brings you joy and happiness. Take care of yourself. If you do not find something positive, you will drive yourself (and possibly others) insane during this ordeal. The next section provides some ideas for reducing stress and practicing self-care.

CHECKLIST FOR
A DOCTOR'S APPOINTMENT

Prior to your doctor's appointment, write down all your questions. Gather all your medical records to take with your appointment.

- ☐ Research the doctor that you are going to see by using the Internet. Google the doctor's name, using websites like Health grades to see what other patients say. The local county clerk's office will have any lawsuits that have been filed against the doctor listed as public information.

- ☐ Create your list of questions prior to your appointment. Make sure you have room to write the answers down on your sheet. KEEP YOUR NOTES!

- ☐ Bring another person with you to the appointment for support. It is always good to have someone else hear what the doctor has to say.

- ☐ You could ask the doctor if you could record the conversation.

- ☐ If a procedure is going to be performed, ask how many of such procedures the doctor has done.

- ☐ Ask for a complete description on what would be done and how. If there is going to be a deviation from what was originally planned for you, how will you be informed of this change?

- ☐ When you are provided with a consent form, make sure you read over it completely. If there is something you don't understand, do not sign it.

- ☐ Do your own research on the diagnosis that you have been given. Make sure the information is provided by an objective party.

- ☐ Find the manufacturer of any hardware that is being used. Research the company through the FDA website. You should be aware of FDA approval or pending approval for the specific use in your condition.

- ☐ If a specific drug is being used, this can also be researched on the FDA website for approval and side effects.

- ☐ The most important thing: *GET A SECOND OPINION*!

CHECKLIST FOR AN ATTORNEY

- ☐ Find an attorney who specializes in your situation.

- ☐ If possible, get a referral from someone you know. If you cannot get a referral, start with phone interviews of potential attorneys.

- ☐ Once you have chosen an attorney to interview, begin by asking how many cases he or she has had like yours. More importantly, how many cases has the attorney won?

- ☐ Ask for the names of clients you can talk with about their experiences with the attorney.

- ☐ Ask how long the attorney has practiced this type of law.

- ☐ Ask if the attorney requires a contingency or retainer fee.

- ☐ Ask how you will know if you have a strong case.

- ☐ Ask what types of technology, databases, etc. the attorney will use for your case.

- ☐ Find out how much interaction there will be between you and the attorney as the case is being worked.

- ☐ Ask about your own responsibilities during the case.

- ☐ Ask if the attorney's personal network includes experts in various fields to draw on as resources.

- ☐ Ask if the attorney has any conflicts of interest with your case.

- ☐ How will the attorney prepare you for a settlement? For example, if you're successful, how will the settlement be disbursed? Who gets paid first? Do you have any say on expenses paid to the attorney? What happens if you lose your case and there is no settlement?

- ☐ If you go to trial, how will you be prepared for the trial?

- ☐ What will it cost you to go to trial?

- ☐ What type of recourse is there for you if the trial doesn't work out the way you expect?

RECORD-KEEPING TEMPLATE

Date	Doctor/Address	Mileage	Comments/Tests

18. MAINTAINING YOUR SANITY— DEALING WITH GUILT, FRUSTRATION, ANGER, AND STRESS

It is true that if you do not find some way to manage the stress during an acute or chronic illness, and certainly once the legal system is involved, you will feel like you are losing your mind. I have found that surrounding yourself with people with whom you can talk openly about how you feel without having to sugar-coat it is critical. You need a sounding board. You need someone who will hold space for you to just cry!

Do not forget to eat! Do not give up your exercise schedule! I did both of these and they caught up with me. Ten pounds later and not recognizing my body one day when I looked in the mirror was devastating to me. Exercise can be one of the best stress relievers there is. It will allow you to release the tension and anger, as well as pain. I have gotten back on the exercise train and am working through the physical and emotional pain that is coming up.

Yoga is a great practice that I learned before my husband's injury and I have returned to it over the past year. It has been one of the many lifesavers for me, both physically and spiritually. It has taught me to slow down and breathe even when I don't want to.

MY SPIRITUAL GROWTH
On a far more personal level, throughout this entire ordeal, I feel like I have not only let my husband and my family down. I am filled with questions and self-doubt. How can I ever trust my instincts again? How does one begin to trust his or her profession? How do I not become a conspiracy theorist? How do I keep from being bitter?

To be truthful, I had difficulty managing my emotions and my life. I am lucky to have a loving family who does not harbor anger or bitterness. I can own enough of my own guilt and will work through my own anger and distrust in this world. We need to begin to heal the wounds that have led us to this place. My mom has always said "God does not close a door without opening another." He has surely opened more doors than I would have imagined during the five years of our journey. I am still trying to figure out the lesson I am to learn through this crazy story.

I still do not understand why, but one day, I met a wonderful man, an angel on a day that I needed one. He came into my life while driving me to the airport one snowy morning in Albany, New York. We talked briefly about my story, and he then began to recite from memory a poem he had written. I cannot repeat it verbatim but I will tell you it was so beautiful and touched my heart completely. He told me he does not publish his poems, but saves them for people he connects with. I felt honored that he had one for me. I knew somewhere in his words was strength and the reality that life would move forward and good would come out of the challenging situation. I believe the Universe has a reason for everything in life and I have encountered many in the past five years.

Today, I can say I am grateful for this experience. I will create something positive out of this situation. I can use this as an opportunity to share my story with others; hopefully they will not make the mistakes I have made. If my words and experiences help even one person, then the many injustices Dennis and our family have suffered have not been for nothing. I have always been a patient advocate; now I am more than just that. I will be the voice for those who cannot speak for themselves.

I discovered that it was important for me to engage in regular spiritual activity. I have always talked with God and believed but there is nothing like a traumatic event to bring you closer and have the desire for a spiritual closeness.

I also turned to acupuncture for my stress relief. Without my acupuncturist, I would not have survived. She also brought me into the world of shamanic healing, a practice that uses Native American or indigenous philosophies to approach healing. I have always had an interest in this type of healing, but neither the time nor devotion to truly embrace the practice. I now practice this daily and we meet monthly to hold space and assist each other in healing journeys for each other. This meditative practice has truly changed my life and has allowed me to feel my anger, but release it when it no longer serves me. I am grounded and for the first time in years, at peace with my life and all that has happened to me in the past six years.

I am also grateful and practice my "attitude of gratitude" on a daily basis. There is life for both the injured and the loved ones after traumatic medical, and legal events, whatever their outcomes. So many heroes entered my life during this time who need to be thanked for supporting my family, for being there when I needed a shoulder or ear to vent to when things just didn't go the way we thought they should. I also need to thank the pharmaceutical company for changing its materials so people have a better understanding of the products.

MOVING ON

We have moved on. Dennis and I are living our lives.

After the second surgery, Dennis was in severe pain every day. Dr. Smith recommended a foraminotomy. During this procedure, a small incision is made in the back to access the spine. A small amount of bone is cut away to make a larger space for the nerves. This releases the pinching on the nerve that ultimately causes the pain.

On March 06, 2013, Dennis underwent the foraminotomy. We were frightened and wondered if this would resolve his pain. Would the feeling in his feet return? Would the sciatica go away? We had no clue what would happen after the surgery, but we were so hopeful.

Dennis prepared for the surgery and had his pre-operative physical the week before. Like any other physical, it was normal.

On March 5, 2013, we received the EKG done the day before—the results showed that Dennis had had an infarct (heart attack). I could not believe my eyes reading the report. There was no way to know when he had a heart attack; he never had any symptoms. His physician and I reviewed his test and thought he could still go ahead with surgery, but after notifying Dr. Smith, the surgeon decided the operation should be put on hold until Dennis could get a cardiology consult.

Dennis was psyched for the surgery, so when he was told he could not have the operation, he was angry and frustrated. He knew he had not had a heart attack. He asked me, "Now what am I going to do? I can't do this. I can't wait."

I felt so bad for him. It took me a few hours to realize one way to determine what was going on was to order an echocardiogram. An echocardiogram, also known as an echo, is a type of ultrasound that uses high-pitched sound waves sent through a device called a transducer. These waves are turned into pictures that can be visualized. The test was ordered right away so the result could be returned quickly and hopefully we could continue with the surgery.

I contacted Dr. Smith to let him know that Dennis's internal medicine doctor thought it was fine to proceed with the surgery as long as the echocardiogram was normal. Dennis was put back on the surgery schedule for March 6, 2013. Now we waited for the cardiologist to call with the results, to see if there had been heart damage or any proof of a heart attack. The call from the cardiologist finally came in at 9:00 p.m. on March 5, 2013. He reported that there was no evidence showing heart damage or signs of a heart attack. Dennis was cleared for surgery, just the news we were waiting for!

Dennis was so pleased and so relieved that there was no evidence of a heart attack and he was back on for the surgery. He returned to psyching himself up for the surgery again. He was scheduled for surgery at 1:00 p.m. the following day. The rest of the night was somber as we both prepared for his third operation. It is hard not to worry about all the unknown things. Neither of us slept very well; it is hard to sleep when there is so much on your mind.

On the morning of March 6, 2013, we both woke and got ready to take Dennis to a hospital one hour away from our home. It was snowing and six to eight inches of snow were expected. Nevertheless, off we went.

We arrived at the hospital and Dennis ended up going into surgery about thirty minutes early. Dr. Smith had a cardiologist visit with Dennis and reviews the results of his EKG and echo before surgery. They all agreed that the EKG was not accurate and that he had not had a heart attack. It is amazing how many times errors are made in medicine. If you did not know what or how to handle the situation, you could be sent down the wrong path. *Always get a second opinion!*

The surgery was started and a three-inch incision was made in Dennis's back along L4-L5 (lumbar vertebrae 4 and 5). The procedure was completed to relieve the pressure from the nerves. Dennis was sent to recovery and monitored for about an hour before he was taken to his room on the surgical floor. He had some pain but nothing he could not handle. He was progressing nicely and by 7:00 p.m., he was up walking around the surgical floor, commenting that he was ready to go home already. He hated being in the hospital, but nevertheless, would have to stay the night. He was able to get up and walk several times that night since he could not sleep. By 9:00 a.m. the following morning, he was released from the hospital and we headed home. He was so happy and relieved. He still had some pain, but it was not as bad as he thought it would be.

He started out on the ride home. The snowstorm was over but the roads were still sloppy. When Dennis arrived home, he was more tired than he thought and in more pain. He was happy to be home and was able to relax. He took a pain pill and lying down, he finally was able to sleep.

Over the next three days, recovery moved along nicely. Dennis used a walker for the first two days and then after that, was able to walk erect—something he had not been able to do in four years. It was around the fifth day of recovery that he realized that he did not have sciatica and that feeling began to return in his feet. By the seventh day, he was walking normally, without limping or dragging his leg. We were so happy and relieved—the third surgery was a charm.

AFTERWORD

Today, as I am writing this, Dennis is six months out of surgery and is still doing well. Dr. Smith is happy with the progress Dennis is making. We truly believe it will continue to improve and healing will continue. He is still totally disabled but he has moments of pain relief now, which is more than he had before the foraminotomy.

Our children are now grown. The older son is 25, our daughter 22, and our youngest son is now 18. They are all doing well and have learned a lot from this situation. They have learned to advocate for themselves, to live within their means, and most importantly, they learned to never take a single day of their life for granted.

Dennis and his brother have worked through their pain and anger. They are not as close as they once were, but they talk and cover one another's backs. Don, Dennis's former employer, and Dennis have not spoken since the incident.

This entire experience has truly become a gift and a second chance for my husband and me. We are better people because of the journey we have taken. What we went through taught our children and us so much. This has made me a better practitioner—one who looks for answers, one who is compassionate about her patient's conditions. I can only hope that this story helps you and your loved ones as well.

APPENDIX:
SOME STATE
WORKER'S COMPENSATION LAWS

(Sources: *West's Encyclopedia of American Law,*
Encyclopedia of Everyday Law: Worker's Compensation)

Worker's compensation laws vary from state to state. It is important for you to understand the laws of your state and how they affect you. Here is a short list of some of the basic rules among the individual states.

- **Alabama**: For temporary or permanent total disability, injured worker receives 66 2/3% of the wages with a minimum and maximum wages established by law. The employer selects the worker's physician.

- **Arizona**: Disability rate is 66 2/3% of the wages with no minimum weekly payments but maximum payments established by law. The worker selects the physician.

- **California**: A state agency oversees the selection of the physician.

- **District of Columbia**: the worker selects the physician from a list created by the District of Columbia.

- **Florida**: After the worker reaches maximum medical improvement, $10 co-pay is required to be paid by the worker for all medical services.

- **Georgia**: Maximum period of temporary total disability payment is 400 weeks.

- **Illinois**: No limit on duration of temporary total disability payments.

- **Iowa**: Disability rate for temporary or permanent total disability is 80 percent of spendable earnings.

- **Kansas**: Temporary total disability is capped at $100,000. Permanent total disability capped at $125, 00. Worker's Compensation benefits are subject to offset for unemployment and social security benefits.

- **Massachusetts**: Disability rate is 60% of wage.

- **Mississippi**: Maximum period of temporary disability is 450 weeks. Cap on temporary total disability is $131,787. Cap on permanent total disability is $136,507.

- **Nevada**: Injured worker can waive the right to worker's compensation.

- **New York**: Disability rate is 66 2/3% of wages. Worker selects physician form state's list of worker's compensation physicians.

- **Oregon**: Duration of temporary disability payments is duration of disability.

- **Texas**: Employers are not required to purchase worker's compensation insurance.

- **West Virginia**: State-funded insurer is the exclusive worker's compensation insurer in West Virginia.

WORKER'S COMPENSATION ADMINISTRATIVE AGENCIES BY STATE

- Alabama: Alabama Department of Industrial Relations
- Alaska: Alaska Division of Worker's Compensation
- Arizona: Industrial Commission of Arizona
- Arkansas: Arkansas Workers Compensation Commission
- California: California Department of Industrial Relations
- Colorado: Colorado Department of Labor and Employment
- Connecticut: State of Connecticut Workers Compensation Commission
- Delaware: State of Delaware Department of Labor, Division of Industrial Affairs
- District of Columbia: DC Department of Employment Services
- Florida: Florida Department of Financial Services
- Georgia: State of Georgia State Board of Workers Compensation
- Hawaii: State of Hawaii Department of Labor and Industrial Relations
- Idaho: Idaho Industrial Commission
- Illinois: Illinois Workers Compensation Commission
- Indiana: Workers Compensation Board of Indiana
- Iowa: Iowa Division of Workers' Compensation
- Kansas: Kansas Department of Labor
- Kentucky: Kentucky Office of Workers' Claims
- Louisiana: Louisiana Works Department of Labor

- Maine: Maine Workers Compensation Board
- Maryland: Maryland Workers Compensation Commission
- Massachusetts: Massachusetts Department of Labor
- Michigan: Michigan Workers Compensation Agency
- Minnesota: Minnesota Department of Labor & Industry
- Mississippi: Mississippi Workers' Compensation Commission
- Missouri: Missouri Department of Labor & Industrial Relations
- Montana: Montana Department of Labor & Industry - Employment Relations
- Nebraska: Nebraska Workers' Compensation Court
- Nevada: Nevada Division of Industrial Relations
- New Hampshire: New Hampshire Department of Labor
- New Jersey: State of New Jersey Department of Labor & Workforce Development
- New Mexico: State of New Mexico Workers Compensation Administration
- New York: New York State Workers Compensation Board
- North Carolina: North Carolina Industrial Commission
- North Dakota: North Dakota Workforce Safety & Insurance
- Ohio: Ohio Bureau of Workers Compensation
- Oklahoma: Oklahoma Workers Compensation Court
- Oregon: Oregon Department of Consumer & Business Services
- Pennsylvania: Pennsylvania Department of Labor & Industry
- Rhode Island: Rhode Island Division of Workers' Compensation

- South Carolina: South Carolina Workers' Compensation Commission

- South Dakota: South Dakota Department of Labor

- Tennessee: Tennessee Department of Labor & Workforce Development

- Texas: Texas Department of Insurance

- Utah: Labor Commission of Utah

- Vermont: State of Vermont, Department of Labor

- Virginia: The Virginia Workers Compensation Commission

- Washington: Washington State Department of Labor and Industries

- West Virginia: West Virginia Offices of the Insurance Commissioner (Regulatory/Claim Oversight)

- Wisconsin: Wisconsin Department of Workforce Development

- Wyoming: State of Wyoming Workers Safety and Compensation Division

BIBLIOGRAPHY AND
ADDITIONAL RESOURCES

American Association of Justice. *The Role of America's Civil Justice System in Protecting Patients' Rights*. Retrieved January 25, 2013, from American Association of Justice: http://www.justice.org/resources/Medical_Negligence_Primer.)

American Medical Association. *American Medical Association Informed Consent*. Retrieved Sept 10, 2011, from American Medical Association : http://www.ama-assn.org/ama/pub/physician-resources/legal-topics/patient-physician-relationship-topics/informed-consent.page

Bad Faith Insurance.org. Retrieved July 05, 2008, from Fight Bad Faith Insurance: www.badifaithinsurance.org

Bal, B. Sonny, M. J. (May 2012). American Academy of Orthopedic Surgeons. Retrieved Aug 2012, from American Academy of Orthopedic Surgeons: http://www.aaos.org/news/aaosnow/may12/managing6.asp

Ben-Nissan, G. H. (2004). *Innovative Bioceramics*. University of Technology, Department of Chemistry, Materials and Forensic Science,. UT.

Congress, U. S. (Oct. 26, 2001). Uniting and Strengthening America by Providing Appropriate Tools Required to Intercept and Obstruct Terrorism (USA PATRIOT ACT) Act of 2001.
Public Law 107–56. Washington, DC, U.S.: 107th Congress.

DeCarlo, Donald T. (2009). Perspectives . Retrieved Feb 23, 2013, from A Verisk Analytics Company: http://www.iso.com/Newsletters/Perspectives/issue-9-article-The-Workers-Compensation-Fraud.html

Drug Information Online. Retrieved Jan 04, 2013, from Drugs.com: http://www.drugs.com/search.php?searchterm=gabapentin

Guyton, Gregory P. (1999). "A Brief History of Worker's Compensation." *Iowa Orthopaedic Journal*, 19, 106-110.

Hartwig, Robert P. (2012). As Labor Markets Recover, Will Workers Compensation Insurers Lag Behind? Divergent Fortunes: Stark Law. (2008-2013, 0 0). Stark Law. Retrieved Feb 15, 2013, from Stark Law: http://starklaw.org/stark_law.htm

Hartwig, R.P. and Wilkinson, Claire (April 2010). *Terrorism Risk: A Reemergent Threat. Impacts for Property/Casualty Insurers*.

History of Worker's Comp. Retrieved July 2009, from US Legal: http://workerscompensation.uslegal.com/history/

Injury and Illness Prevention Programs. Occupational Safety and Health Administration . U.S. Department of Labor.

International Risk Management. (2000-13). IRMI State Administrative Agencies . Retrieved Feb 25, 2013, from IRMI: http://www.irmi.com/resources/categories/statewcagencies.aspx

Katz, T. L. (April, 2000). Hate Crimes Against Humanity. (T. O. Register, Producer) Retrieved October 18, 2010, from Sweet Liberty.org: http://www.sweetliberty.org/issues/hate/bodybrokers.htm

Laurence, Beth J. (July 2006). *How Do You Start the Worker's Comp Process?* Retrieved July 2007, from http://www.disabilitysecrets.com/workmans-comp : http://www.disabilitysecrets.com/workmans-comp-question-18.html

Manning, W. L. (1996). Summary of the Medicare and Medicaid Patient Protection Act of 1987 (42 U.S.C. 1320a-7b). Retrieved Jan. 20, 2013, from *Physician Financial Relationships With Others*: http://www.netreach.net/~wmanning/fasumm.htm

Mercola, D. (Feb. 2011). *Take care of your health*. Retrieved Feb 23, 2013, from Mercola.com : http://articles.mercola.com/sites/articles/archive/2011/02/04/death-by-medicine-an-update.aspx

Mulloy, D. F., & Hughes., R. G. (2010). "Wrong-Site Surgery: A Preventable Medical Error." In D. F. Mulloy & R. G. Hughes., *NCBI Resources Bookshelf*. Bethesda , Maryland, U.S.: National Center for Biotechnology Information.

National Association of Insurance Commissioners. (2006). Worker's Compensation Large Deductible Study. Kansas City , MO, US: NAIC Products & Services Division.

Occupational Injury Report. Washington State Labor.

Whiton, A. (n.d.). Ezine. Retrieved 12 05, 2007, from Article Source: http://EzineArticles.com/7226188: http://ezinearticles.com/?Decreasing-Workmens-Compensation-Expenses&id=7226188

Williams Law Group. (2013). (W. L. Group, Producer) Retrieved Feb. 21, 2013, from Keith Williams Law Group: http://www.keithwilliamslawgroup.com/library

ABOUT THE AUTHOR

D r. Debra Muth is a doctor who has literally healed herself. During her twenties, serious health problems began to interfere with her career. After a string of mainstream doctors failed to help her, Debra began investigating natural medicine to restore her health. The many holistic disciplines she discovered improved her health so dramatically that she earned credentials in them in order to help others.

Dr. Muth's credentials include:

- Naturopathic Doctor (ND)

- Women's Health Nurse Practitioner (WHNP)

- Board Certified Anti-Aging Specialist (BAAHP)

- Lyme Literate Practitioner for treatment of chronic Lyme disease

She has been in active practice for more than seventeen years. She is well respected by her patients and colleagues for treating her patients as individuals. Dr. Muth is also is a Board Certified Anti-Aging Specialist through the American Academy of Anti-Aging & Regenerative Medicine (A4M), an organization of which she has been a member for several years.

Debra is a sought-after and renowned speaker in complimentary medicine. She has over seventeen years of clinical and practice management experience. She presents postgraduate seminars for health care professionals nationwide throughout the year. She also provides seminars to the general public in the management of male and female hormonal therapy, osteoporosis, and weight loss.

She is a contributing author to Stephanie Moran's book *Audacious Aging*, as well as being the creator of two separate CD recordings entitled "Hormones, Hormones, Hormones", and "How Your Thyroid Works" that provide you with everything you need to know about treating these conditions.

Please visit her website for more information:
www.serenitywellness.com